Beyond the Prison

Gathering Dreams of Freedom

D0556946

edited by

David Denborough

with contributions from

**Rosemary Couch, Clint Deveaux
Eddie Ellis, Harold Gatensky
Sharon Gollan, Blanche Hampton
Ray Jackson, Sheridan Linnell
Mishka Lysack, Marilyn O'Neill
Trevor Pugh, Gaye Stockell, Pia van de Zandt
Women and Political Action Forums
WOWSafe (Women of the West for Safe Families)**

DULWICH CENTRE PUBLICATIONS
Adelaide, South Australia

published by
Dulwich Centre Publications
Hutt St PO Box 7192
Adelaide, South Australia 5000
phone (61-8) 8223 3966

cover artwork by
Suzy Stiles and Loretta Geuenich

printed and manufactured in Australia by
Graphic Print Group, Richmond, South Australia

Contents

Contents (cont'd)

Acknowledgements

The creation of this book has only been possible due to the long histories of resistance to prisons in this country, and the struggles of the feminist movement to address men's violence. As with most work in relation to prisons in this land, the initial impetus came from Indigenous Australians. Those who were involved in the 'Reclaiming Our Stories, Reclaiming Our Lives' Project (see *Dulwich Centre Newsletter*, 1995, No.1) invited white Australians to further investigate prisons, their role in ongoing injustice, and to explore ways beyond.

Dulwich Centre Publications created the opportunities for travel to North America, Aotearoa/New Zealand and within Australia to visit those communities that are challenging current trends of imprisonment. David Denborough travelled to the USA and Aotearoa/New Zealand in August 1995, Cheryl White and David Denborough travelled to North America in April 1996, and Jane Hales, Cheryl White and David Denborough travelled within Australia in July 1996. Geoff Miller was instrumental in introducing the work of Indigenous Australians within Alice Springs and the surrounding areas. The conversations and collective learnings that were generated on these trips acted as a foundation for this publication.

The content of much of this book has been provided by the following people who contributed their time, energy, experiences and ideas through interviews and/or writings: *Rosemary Couch, Clint Deveaux, Eddie Ellis, Harold Gatensky, Sharon Gollan, Blanche Hampton, Ray Jackson, Sheridan Linnell, Mishka Lysack, Marilyn O'Neill, Trevor Pugh, Gaye Stockell, Pia van de Zandt, Women and Political Action Forums: Marg McHugh, Carol Johnston, Jo Hawke and Suzanne Elliott, and WOWSafe (Women of the West for Safe Families).* (See contributors' pages at the end of this book.)

Many others contributed their time and learnings either through interviews, conversations and/or writings: *Tim Anderson, Jim Consedine, Stephen Donaldson, Cheryl Gysin, Elijah Ingram, Wayne Jones, Danny Mendoza, Geoff Miller, Barbara Nicholson, Loretta Perry, George Prendes,*

Juan Rivera.

With these wide-ranging contributions, David Denborough wove together a first draft and a series of feedback sessions were held. The ideas of the following people resulted in a major refiguring of the publication: *Maggie Carey, Suzanne Elliot, Loretta Geuenich, Sharon Gollan, Rob Hall, Brother Henry, Alan Jenkins, Ian Law, Laurie Lever, Alison Newton, Penni Revel, Vanessa Swan, Claire Ralfs, Brother Stephen, Pam Schofield, Suzy Stiles, and the WOWSafe women.*

Chris McLean spent hours over the first draft and revised its entire structure, and Jane Hales made detailed suggestions and improvements.

In July 1996 in Adelaide, South Australia, two 'Beyond Prisons' workshops were held. The conversations that took place during these workshops led to a rethinking and reworking of parts of the text.

David Denborough gathered together a second draft and, in August 1996, Chris McLean, David Weaver, Yvonne Sliep, Michael White and Cheryl White offered considerable feedback and ideas. Together, Cheryl White and David Denborough then worked thoroughly on the draft to bring this publication to its current form.

Throughout the process Cherice Ogilvie and Linda Higgins offered challenges on issues of class and contributed hours of practical work. In the publication stage, Jane Hales typeset this book. Melissa Raven proofread it and acted as copy editor. Margaret Wild and Linda Higgins read it through. Suzy Stiles designed the cover, Loretta Geuenich provided artwork, and Cath Muscat photography.

This book began as a newsletter and evolved as a collective project of Dulwich Centre Publications. It is the result of many people's contributions, from many different communities, and builds upon long histories of prison protest.

Dulwich Centre Publications

Editor's personal acknowledgements

The part that I have played in this publication would not have been possible without the challenges, friendship and support of many others. The following people helped to balance my sense of outrage, sorrow and hope while I worked within Australian prisons from 1993-1996. Firstly, my friend Deirdre

Hyslop, who continues to care behind prison walls, who brings colour, light and laughter to a world in which it is often missing, and secondly, Tony Magers, without whom I might never have begun to work within prisons, and who continues to walk beside me.

Inside the prisons, there are many to acknowledge. The following men are still incarcerated - I am unsure of the potential repercussions if they were named fully in this publication: 'The Rollercoasters' (Steve, Gary, Barry, Bob, Dave, John, Marshall, Don, Glen & Todd) who invited me to share stories and create song; and Bob, Gary, Barry, John, Ken, Danny, Brett and Kevin, who let me know that I am a squarehead and who offered me hope of meaningful, respectful dialogue. John W, whose letter to maintain connection will forever remain with me; John M, whose gentle trust honoured me; Archie, whose challenges and fire are still alive in my head; Bob, whose openness created pathways for me to travel; and Shane, whose energy and determination behind prison walls sustained my sense of hope. Todd Gordon, with whom I shared laughter, frustrations and heartache, who taught me through friendship and opened my heart to new ways of seeing. Vicky Barrett, who showed me how spirits and sharing stories can bring us together; and Russell Sykes, whose determination and strength moved me on when my soul needed lifting. Cheryl Gysin, who offered me the strength of survival; and Wayne Jones, who continues to show me that it is possible to unlock hearts of caged steel and to create friendship across lifetimes of difference.

Throughout my travels many people offered warmth, hospitality and ideas including Lorraine Grieves and the Anti-Anorexia and Bulimia League of Vancouver, Canada, Richard Chasin and Laura Chasin, Lucia Gaton, Sarah Hughes and Bailey, Michael Kimmel, Terry Kupers, Stephen Madigan, Don Sabo, and David Walls.

In the midst of it all occurred two important events: Victor Lewis, in *The Color of Fear* (Stir-Fry Productions, 1991), reached my soul with his outrage and demanded that I ask myself what it means to be white; and the Port Elliot gathering (see *Dulwich Centre Newsletter*, 1995, No.4) reminded me of the power to our journeys.

When it came time to write, the following people offered me a sense of homecoming: Samantha Brazel, Maggie Carey, Michael Flood, Jenny Kitchin, Samantha Lee, Chris McLean, Cath Muscat, David Newman, Penni Revel, Niamh Nic Stiofan, Michelle Swift and Mark Trudinger.

Throughout and always, Ginna McElhany's friendship lifted my spirits; Jane Hales' faith and song sustained me; and Cheryl White, while challenging and laughing, offered me a sense of companionship in the world. My family continued to create space for me to imagine other ways of living and set the example of taking risks in order to get there. They took me under their wing when I needed it, and at the same time Erica Denborough and Michael Denborough tirelessly read through and edited reams of early drafts. Without the histories within my family of love, support and challenging convention, I would never have had the faith nor the imagination to have played my part in the creation of this book.

Finally, it is important for me to acknowledge that half-way through the process of editing this publication I was overwhelmed with the powerlessness and despair of prisons and could see little good in the world. Were it not for the community response of people in Adelaide, and the friendship of Cheryl White who largely facilitated this response and supported me through this time, issues of prisons might have remained tearing within me. Bringing them into the open and sharing them as collective issues has opened the possibilities for action.

I believe that many people are affected by prisons in deeply personal and powerful ways. I hope this book brings some of the outrage, sorrow and dilemmas associated with prisons out into the light so that we do not have to struggle with them in isolation. I hope it also offers the sparks for change, radical change, for it is from a collective belief in these possibilities that the following stories have been recorded and this book created.

DD

Editor's dilemmas

In putting together this publication I have tried to avoid the detachment that so often accompanies discussions or writings about prison. Prisons are about people, their lives, experiences and stories. The first section of this book attempts to give voice to the experiences of those most affected by prison. This has raised a number of dilemmas. Having never been imprisoned, how could I, as a white middle-class man, from a position of enormous privilege, try to convey the experience of within, from the outside? I have struggled to give voice to stories that convey the experience of prison in ways that avoid the potential appropriation of these stories and the lives of others.

I have also tried to write in ways that are not detached, that offer you, the reader, my company, and that put myself in the picture. This has also brought questions. How could I reflect the dilemmas of my own position in this culture and my experience in relation to prisons, the good and the bad, in ways that acknowledge the privilege from which these experiences have been born? The reactions, dilemmas and experiences of professionals like me seem, on the one hand, so trivial and potentially trivialising of other people's experiences and, on the other, important to be explored and named. The following pages are the product of these dilemmas.

Issues of Gender

From 1993 to 1996 I worked within an Australian men's maximum security prison. The experiences I had during that time, and particularly the injustices I witnessed and participated within, have acted as the foundations from which I have put together this book. The following pages, in exploring the experience of prison, the practices of imprisonment, and the beliefs and attitudes that allow us to imprison, focus primarily on men's experience and masculine ways of being. Prisons represent to me an institutional regime of the worst extremes of dominant masculine culture. I hope this book can play a part in exposing their practices of degradation and exploring ways to move beyond.

Women make up approximately five percent of prison populations. The experiences of women within prisons, their acts of resistance, women's histories and current struggles offer alternative ways of understanding imprisonment. These are not explored at any depth within these pages, and are instead to be the subject of an upcoming publication from Dulwich Centre Publications.

DD

Introduction

This book is part of a broader project intended to break the cultural silences that surround prisons and imprisonment. In this country this project has long histories. From Indigenous Australian resistance, to convict protest, to the present day, individuals, groups and communities have gathered to name the realities of prisons, to name the outrage and sorrow as well as the stories of survival.

This land from which I write was invaded to become a prison, not only for the Indigenous peoples but also for the poor of Britain. Our lives have been built upon histories of imprisonment and institutions of degradation. Now, over two hundred years later, it is still the poor and Indigenous Australians who fill the prisons within our cities.

I wonder what it means to live in a country with these histories. How does it affect our attitudes to prison to grow up in this land, in the shadow of such stories? In my own life, exploring these questions has led me to uncover a personal history that was once silenced - a history of struggling to come to terms with prisons, a history of uncomfortableness about imprisonment, a history, no matter how slight, of protest. I wonder if this would also be true for others.

It has only been in the process of putting together this book that I came to hear that my great-grandfather was imprisoned in Ghent, Belgium, for an unknown crime and for an unknown sentence. Similarly it was only recently that I thought at any length about the life of a great-great-grandfather. He was the first Chief Justice of this country, and I now realise that he sat in judgement over others, mostly poor settlers, the families of ex-convicts, and Indigenous Australians, and sentenced many of them to prison, and some to death. In my own life I recall visiting one of Australia's ex-institutions of torture, a place of brandings, whippings, and sensory deprivation, that has now been turned into a tourist attraction. I remember walking through this old prison and standing in the solitary confinement cell. I closed the door on myself to try to imagine what life must have been like inside and I could not conceive of how some people could do this to other people. This image haunted me as I imagine it must haunt many children in this country. That was for me, in hindsight, the beginning of my history of prison protest. Later, as my father and older sister were arrested on numerous occasions demonstrating for nuclear disarmament or other related issues, prisons loomed a little closer, and the absurdity and arbitrary nature of the law became more clear.

Three and a half years ago I began working within a maximum security men's prison. My privilege had allowed me to remain largely unaware of the realities of life behind the razor wire but, once there, I came to realise that the historical institutions of torture, which had haunted me in my early years, in many ways still existed. It became clear that within this country, my country, in every city, there stand institutions of degradation, institutions designed to punish and break the spirit of those within them. It also became clear that inside are the poor, the young, and the Indigenous peoples of this country, in the majority of cases for non-violent crimes.

I recall standing in the centre of the prison in which I worked, after lockdown, hearing the sounds of prisoners in their cells seemingly so far away, and knowing that the chances of me ever being incarcerated were minuscule. The utter injustice of the 'justice system' overwhelmed me. Standing in the centre of the prison was one thing; trying to raise the issues with those outside was another, particularly when it came to talking about men's violence. While I was working within the prison system, many of the women and some of the men I was closest to had experienced the brutality of men's violence and together we were beginning to make a stand on these issues. I was often leaving the prison to attend Men Against Sexual Assault meetings, or to work with young men in schools around issues of gender and violence.

Working within the prison and in schools was often exhilarating. When we'd make videos in the prison to show in the schools, it felt like partnerships were beginning to be formed. However, with prisons often seen as an appropriate response to men's violence, at times I could feel as if I was drowning within two torrents of water. Within one was the devastation, grief and outrage of men's violence. Within the other was the brutality of prisons, their sorrow and hopelessness. I had few opportunities to talk with people about what it means to live in a culture where men's violence is endemic and devastating, and where our major response to these crimes is to involve the police and prisons. If these torrents of water are brought to oppose one another, as they so often are in discussions about either men's violence or prisons, there is, to my mind, only a sense of desolation.

This book is an attempt to find ways in which these torrents of water, rather than being brought to oppose each other, can instead find ways to join, to carve new ways forward. In the hope of finding ways beyond the prison and building a culture in which institutions of torture are no longer acceptable in our cities, this book seeks to explore not only the injustices currently directed at working-class and Indigenous Australian communities, but also issues of men's violence.

In my own experience these issues are powerful and deeply personal. Over recent months I have been privileged to hear of people's histories of prison protest, or struggles around issues of prison. So many of our stories seem to have remained silent. I wonder what would occur if our stories of connection to prison, their sorrow, outrage and dilemmas were brought out into the light. This book is an attempt to invite these conversations.

It is also an attempt to share conversations that have already taken place. In the process of putting together these pages I have walked through landscapes of sorrow and landscapes of joy. I have sat within the most desolate of institutions and spoken with the most optimistic of people. I have heard both the wailing *and* the singing behind prison walls. I have spoken with communities who are claiming back their lives and loved ones from systems of degradation, and I have seen what is often hidden. I have witnessed voices of resistance flowing in even the most sterile, soulless places.

I invite you to sit within these places. I hope that we can walk together through prison hospitals, the yards, the cells, and the daily grind of prison life. It is so easy to shut down when reading of places of injustice and inhumanity. I have tried to write in a way that offers you my company, for if we are together, perhaps our hearts will remain open.

Part One of this book, entitled *Songs of Survival*, seeks to explore the experiences of those incarcerated, their families, and workers within prison. It also includes the voices of women who have experienced men's violence and their interactions with the criminal 'justice' system.

Part Two is entitled *Exploring the Politics of Imprisonment.* To most, who have never caught a glimpse of life behind the razor wire, prisons are a 'necessary evil' to protect our community, to punish wrong-doers, and prevent further crime. But prisons are much more than a reactive response to crime. Prisons are creators of meanings and identities. They give life to certain interpretations and they take lives away. This section explores the politics of imprisonment - who it is that we lock away, which communities are torn apart by imprisonment, and how this is justified. It explores the ways in which notions of punishment saturate our culture, and discusses in some detail the dilemmas regarding responding to men's violence.

Part Three is entitled *Beyond the Prison.* There are rich histories of prison resistance. There are people, both inside and outside, working day and night trying to give voice to the realities of prisons and trying to create alternatives. They are almost exclusively from cultures and communities that have experienced the police and prisons as tools of colonisation. This section attempts to convey the invitations that they offer us. Invitations to create new ways of righting wrongs. Invitations to create, with them, new culture and in the process to address the wrongs committed against Indigenous Australians.

I hope that the voices in this section challenge and spark the imagination. I believe that they invite us to imagine a 'justice system' based on moving forwards, towards connection, towards restoration of the damage done. I believe that they invite us to refuse to replicate domination, to instead create places, processes and symbols of hope, and to imagine approaches to crime that, instead of tearing neighbourhoods apart, rebuild relationships and communities.

Through these invitations, the outrage and utter sorrow of prisons can turn instead to dreams of freedom. This country from which I write was invaded to become a prison. We have unique histories. This land knows of prisons like no other. It knows of the sorrow and the violence, and it knows of dreaming. Dreams of freedom lie scattered in the most unexpected of places. It seems time to gather them together.

Songs of Survival

The following pages invite you to catch a glimpse of life in prison. They describe the solitude, the violence, and the sorrow of prisons, but also the ways in which men and women who are incarcerated survive these institutions. It is easy to be overwhelmed by the destructiveness of prisons, and yet to see only the brutality is to ignore much of the experience of those behind the razor wire: their daily resistance, the ways they fashion lives and relationships in the face of the overwhelming degradation.

This section has evolved as a collection of writings by prisoners, ex-prisoners, families of prisoners, and workers within prison, which I have laced together with occasional reflections informed by my conversations with those inside.

1

Glimpses of life
in prison

Across the silence

[It takes courage] ... *to put into words an experience which was, for most*
of us, something we dealt with overtly, but felt at our deepest levels to be
a nightmare. This is sometimes belied by the apparent lack of emotion
with which [we] ... *discuss the events which transpired during ...*
incarceration. Emotional withdrawal and cynicism are survival tools in
the prison system, used in dealing with the bureaucracy, other inmates
and even family members. Being released doesn't guarantee the
resurfacing of emotional vulnerability, either at the time or even years
later ... At a personal level, the larger issues of brutality and
mistreatment evoke little response from me beyond frustration at the
waste of resource involved. Some small things, like the memory of
carrying foil-covered paper dinner plates up to reception for the women
who would be received at the prison that day, always makes me cry.
(Hampton 1993, p.xvii)

As Blanche Hampton describes in *Prisons and Women*, the book she
edited after serving time within New South Wales prisons[1], it is rare to hear
prisoners or ex-prisoners speak of their time inside. Telling the stories of
incarceration places great demands on those who speak out, as Somebody's
Daughter Theatre Company, a group comprised of women who have served

time in Australian prisons, describe:

> *It's difficult to tell you how I feel. It's difficult to explain the overwhelming sense of betrayal, suffocation and violation. It's difficult for me to tell you I felt defeated. It's difficult to share my secrets and thus share my pain ...* (Rikki & Janai, in Somebody's Daughter Theatre Company 1994, p.56)

There are many obstacles for prisoners or ex-prisoners to tell their stories of prison survival. For one thing, the probation and parole system, an extension of 'corrective' services into the lives of released prisoners for up to three years after release, is seen to encourage a public silence. As part of parole conditions, ex-prisoners are often not allowed to mix with other 'known offenders', others who have been in prison - 'even then the fear of reprisal lingers' (Hampton 1993, p.xvii). Despite the obstacles, some try to build bridges across the silence to convey the experience of incarceration to those outside.

The first night

> *The first night in jail on every sentence is always the worst. The first night in the cell, off the bus, 'Why did I have to do this, get in here?'* (Steve Morgan,[2] in conversation, 1995).

When a person first enters prison they are put through a reception process. They are strip-searched, given a number and prison issue clothing and placed in a cell.

Freedom lost

> *1.16 am. I lie awake on my bed, listening to the sounds of the night. I cannot sleep, even though I want to. This is the worst time in the day for me. This is the time when I realise just where I am. It is the silence that does it. No-one else is awake, or if they are they make no sound. That's when the noises come. The worst torture imaginable, the sounds of freedom. A dog barking somewhere outside the walls, the sounds of buses and cars driving along the main road, right past the jail walls, and off in the distance the sharp, shrill sound of a car alarm as someone seeks cheap room and board in the cell next door. I lie here in the*

darkness, surrounded by stone walls, listening to the sounds of freedom.
Still awake. 1.19 am. (David Pike, 1994, p.19)

With freedom lost, Mumia Abu Jamal, an African American journalist now incarcerated in the US,[3] describes the feelings of waste, hopelessness and timelessness of prisons as 'spirit death':

That prisons are hotbeds of violence is undeniable, but overt expressions of violence are rarely daily ones. The most profound horror of prisons lives in the day-to-day banal occurrences that turn days into months, and months into years, and years into decades. Prison is a second-by-second assault on the soul, a day-to-day degradation of the self, an oppressive steel and brick umbrella that transforms seconds into hours and hours into days. While a person is locked away in distant netherworlds, time seems to stand still; but it doesn't of course. Children left outside grow into adulthood, often having children of their own. Once loving relationships wither into yesterday's dust. Relatives die, their loss mourned in silent loneliness. Times, temperaments, mores change, and the caged move to outdated rhythms ... The mind-numbing, soul-killing savage sameness that makes each day an echo of the day before, with neither thought nor hope of growth, makes prison the abode of spirit death that it is for over a million men and women now held in US hellholes. (Abu-Jamal 1995, pp.64-65)

Men and women incarcerated in prison wake at the same time each day, get locked in at the same time, eat the same foods, see the same walls, and are counted two or three times a day. The sounds of radios, televisions, rattling of keys and clanging of doors fill all the spaces within the prison each day and well into the night. At the same time in many ways those in prison cease to be seen as people - their bodies, sexuality, name, time, opinions, are somehow no longer theirs. Prison uniform is their only clothing and they are 'mustered' like cattle now. There are constant but subtle signs that they are no longer worthy - that they are criminal, bad, not worth the effort.

Suffocation

Listen, the halls are not wide enough
I can touch each side
With my arms outstretched

I tell you there is not enough air in here
Not enough air.
(Sin, in Faith 1993, p.134)

Men and women prisoners know that they are possibly under surveillance at any time and this adds to the claustrophobia. Each prisoner becomes 'their own best guard' (Faith 1993, p.146). Whether in the newest 'designer' prisons or behind archaic sandstone walls, prisoners speak of the suffocation and craving for the feeling of rain on their face.

Resisting the degradation

Scammin', always scammin'. The more rules, the more ways 'round
them. If I go to the clinic, I can get over to activities, unless that prick on
the yard gate sees me. If I can make it to the library, I can get out to the
field when the workers go through. If I get into the clinic yard with the
methadonians, maybe Fred'll whack up with his 'done, or I can stand
over some c..t for his. Anyway, I can get some pills for me headache. I
can get out to see the wing screw to get him to ring reception, so that I
can get those trackpants out of me property. And when I get out for that
phone-call, I'll see Bob in the workers' wing and maybe score some pot.
(Anderson 1992, p.217)

In a context of utter powerlessness, where prisoners can never be guaranteed a straight answer, for many, resistance is a process of gleaning any extra scrap, any tiny privilege that can be wrought from the system. Despite all attempts to rob those in prison of the ways they know themselves, despite the uniformity of clothing and use of numbers and surnames, walking in through any prison the ways in which men and women who are incarcerated assert their individuality are instantly recognisable - each piece of clothing worn slightly differently, the tattoos, the trademark space demarcated for different people, different groups. The use of weights and sports, the sculpting of bodies, the building of physical strength to match the mental, the taking and trading of drugs, the short-term joy and exhilaration, are all daily rituals of resistance.

Study

In jail you get some good training. I mean it's quite an educational
place. I was so naive when I went there, when I was 15 years old, and

then once I got in, boy the next thing I knew how to write phoney cheques and I knew how to open safes and I knew how to trick people and con them out of their money. Man, oh man, you learn a lot of things in there.

We call our institutions in this land correction centres. I don't know why they call it that. You know we live in such a contradictory world, nothing is being corrected there, nothing at all. If anything it should be called what my brother termed it - a corruption centre, for that's where we send our young people, that's where we send those people less fortunate, just go there to be corrupted, go there to be made bitter, go there to become completely dependent on the institution. (Harold Gatensky, in conversation, 1996)

Harold Gatensky served time in Canadian prisons and is now involved in alternative Circle Justice initiatives in the Yukon which he describes in detail in chapter 17. Here he describes how, for many prisoners, study becomes a way of looking forwards, of occupying time. Occasionally this occurs through the education services provided. Far more common, however, is learning 'how not to get caught next time'. Swapping secrets with other prisoners is a crucial part of doing time within prisons, the universities of crime, the centres of corruption.

Surveillance

'I have to watch you take your clothes off.' They took each piece of clothing off me and they checked over each item of clothing and then they said to me, 'Bend over', and I had to bend over. It's worse than having a baby or a medical, that's the honest truth, because you've got no dignity when you're behind bars. You're all theirs, your body is theirs. (Lilly, in Hampton 1993, p.42)

Many women prisoners speak of the ways in which the loss of control and the everyday bodily humiliations often carry added meanings for women. Somebody's Daughter Theatre Company describe how, when women are strip-searched by male officers, or even forced to spend time within men's prisons, such as Jika Jika in Victoria, Australia, the situation can be worse still:

In Jika Jika women prisoners had to have showers in front of up to 5 male officers, with absolutely no privacy, all see through glass - which they said was for security reasons. We had to be strip-searched by male officers if there was no female officers available, which there hardly ever was. If you refused on the grounds of common decency, because you may have had your monthly periods or any other reasons, then you were brutally and forcibly held down by 5 or 6 male officers, by your arms and legs at the same time, then your clothes were completely ripped off you - your legs kicked open and held, your buttocks parted, then vice versa when you were turned over. If you had a tampon in and refused to take it out, because of your pride and dignity, then you were soon stripped of that also, as they would just rip it out themselves. Now I don't know what people call that kind of behaviour outside of prison walls but I call it rape without penetration. (Somebody's Daughter Theatre Company 1994, p.34)

Until late 1994, women prisoners in Victoria, Australia, who were being internally examined in outside hospitals, could be required to wear handcuffs during examinations which took place in front of an officer. Now it's in front of the officer without handcuffs (Women and Imprisonment Group 1995, p.64).

Alone

In the midst of darkness, this little one was a light ray. Tiny, with a Minnie Mouse voice, this daughter of my spirit had finally made the long trek westward, into the bowels of this man-made hell, situated in the south-central Pennsylvania boondocks ... She burst into the tiny visiting room, her brown eyes aglitter with happiness; stopped, stunned, staring at the glassy barrier between us, and burst into tears at this arrogant attempt at state separation. In milliseconds, sadness and shock shifted into fury as her petite fingers curled into tight fists, which banged and pummelled the Plexiglas barrier, which shuddered and shimmied but didn't shatter.

'Break it! Break it!' she screamed. Her mother, recovering from her shock, bundled up Hamida in her arms, as sobs rocked them both. My eyes filled to the brim. My nose clogged.

Her unspoken words echoed in my consciousness: 'Why can't I hug him? Why can't we kiss? Why can't I sit in his lap? Why can't we touch? Why not?'

I turned away to recover. (Abu-Jamal 1995, p.25)

As Mumia Abu-Jamal describes, those in prison experience daily humiliations cut off from those that they love and visits can be haunting experiences that place considerable strain on many relationships. On the other hand, it is a common theme that relationships with people outside provide enormous sustenance for prisoners. Letters and phone calls act as life-lines to another world and photographs or drawings of children often cover cell walls, particularly in women's prisons.

Mothers in prison

> *My baby was three months old*
> *Three years ago.*
> *He calls his Grandma 'Mommy'.*
> *My daughter just turned six.*
> *She calls Aunt Marilyn*
> *'Mommy'.*
> *My children do not know me.*
> *I haven't seen my husband's face*
> *Or heard his voice*
> *In these three years.*
> *I don't know when*
> *I stopped loving him.*
> *I can't love a stranger.*
> (Diane, in Faith 1993, p.211)

The imprisonment of mothers has many ripples. For many women prisoners much of their time revolves around their children. Their responsibilities for their families don't stop. When care-givers ring them up with difficulties, imprisoned mothers have to deal with them from behind bars. There is a dominant story amongst workers in prisons (predominantly male) which states that women prisoners are much more 'demanding and manipulative' than men. Such stories reflect dominant masculine beliefs about women which are widespread throughout the general community. Their effects are to dismiss women's experiences and malign their motives, thus effectively disempowering them. As Blanche Hampton describes:

> *Women are seen as manipulative because they have to be, the system*
> *sets it up. Your child is sick and you want to make a phone call. The*
> *officer in your wing is not going to let you for whatever reason. So you*

think, I'll go to the clinic, and on the way back I'll nip into education, welfare, the psychologist, whoever's got a phone, and I'll get them to do it. One of them isn't there, the other says 'I'll do it later'. You panic and think, 'What if they forget?' So you leave a message for one, ask another one. By then you've asked three people in your anxiety. They then talk amongst themselves and find you've asked them all and so you get written off as manipulative. What on earth are you supposed to do? (in conversation, 1995)

Overcrowding

With overcrowding now the norm in prisons throughout Australia and the USA, those in prison share their cell, the size of a bathroom, every day of the year, with no respite, with someone whose company they do not choose. So extreme are rates of incarceration becoming in the USA that women prisoners in Sybil Brand Jail in Los Angeles sleep in dormitories holding between 130 and 156 people (The Human Rights Watch, cited in Christie 1993, p.91). Under such circumstances there is no privacy, extremely limited access to showers and bathrooms, and enormous potential for violence.

Violence

Prisons are institutions of violence. Violence directed at prisoners by prison guards is far less common than it once was, although in some institutions, especially within large isolated US prisons, it is still endemic. With such power over prisoners, and within an atmosphere of degradation, it seems abuses from officers are in some way inevitable.

Various kinds of state-sponsored torture and abuse - of the kind ingeniously designed to cause pain but without a telltale 'significant injury' - lashing prisoners with leather straps, whipping them with rubber hoses, beating them with naked fists, shocking them with electric currents, asphyxiating them short of death, intentionally exposing them to undue heat or cold, or forcibly injecting them with psychosis-inducing drugs - techniques, commonly thought to be practised outside this nation's borders, are hardly unknown within this nation's prisons. (Supreme Court Justice Harry A. Blackmun, Hudson vs McMillian, 25 February 1992, in Consedine 1993, p.65)

Prisoner violence

Every morning you wake up, if you haven't got somebody to be with ... to put you under their wing ... to look after you, every day you wake up and when the door opens you've got to think of strategies in your head to cope with the day. What's your little plan you're going to use today to keep them from trying to capture you? From putting work on you, or getting you in a position ... every morning you wake up ... what's your little plan today?[4]

Within Australian prisons by far the most common forms of violence now occur between prisoners. Within a context of powerlessness, hierarchies form within the prisoner population. For those low in such hierarchy - young offenders, first-timers, the physically small or weak, every day can be a quest for survival. This is especially true within ultra-masculine institutions. In 1995, within the reception and induction centre of a New South Wales prison, a number of groups were run with transgender inmates. The quote above and the one below are from these groups. Those who experience the violence of other prisoners find themselves in an impossible situation:

For your own best interest you keep your mouth shut. It's the same with rape. If you report the incident you're a dog [prison informer]. *It's all right for guys to sexually assault you and to split you and for you to have to have 12 stitches inserted in you but it's not all right for you to want some sort of dignity back in your life. If you do you're a dog. You're in a catch-22 situation. You've got to keep your mouth shut, you've got to cop it sweet or you know the complications.*

With prisoners needing to remain silent, the extent of violence within prisons is unknown. In the USA, extrapolations of the most reliable research estimate that well over three hundred thousand sexual assaults of male prisoners and over five thousand sexual assaults of women prisoners take place behind bars annually (Donaldson 1995, p.2).[5]

In Australia there has been only one study into the incidence of sexual assault in prison. In 1994, in New South Wales, David Heilpern found that a quarter of young men surveyed said they had been sexually assaulted while in prison (Heilpern 1994, p.4). Of 183 male prisoners aged 18 to 25 who were surveyed, 11 said they were 'rarely' sexually assaulted, 17 said they were occasionally assaulted, 14 said they were assaulted weekly, and two said they were assaulted daily. The study involved 10 women prisoners, three of whom reported occasional sexual assault, and five reported occasional other assault.

Such a climate of sexual violence becomes more disturbing when the experience of those in prison who were sexually abused as children is acknowledged. It is widely recognised that large numbers of women prisoners have experienced such abuse (Faith 1993, p.150). The same seems true for many male prisoners:

> *I think you'd find that the number of men in prison who've been sexually assaulted as children is a lot higher than you would ever imagine. Especially those that have come from boys' homes. It's a dark kept secret. I think it's why people hate rock-spiders [child molesters] so much, but it's not just that. I think the hatred that is caused by being molested in boys' homes is the hatred that makes people commit some crimes against society. Especially when welfare took the kid that was being molested and put him in an institution where he was abused again.*
> (Steve Morgan, in conversation 1995)

Suicide

> *I can see people reaching out every day of the week for help but nobody reaches back, nobody recognises the signs, and if they do they don't act on them. Even when they do recognise that someone is about to commit suicide, rather than helping them move forwards they just chuck them in a dry cell where they've got more time to brood. When I've been really depressed about things and they've put me down in the hospital, all it's made me is more depressed. You've got nothing, no letters, no cigarettes, all you do is give a person another twenty reasons why they should commit suicide.* (a prisoner who chooses to remain anonymous, in conversation, July 1995)

It is seen as a normal reaction for prisoners to be suicidal within the first 24 hours of the reception process. In prisons throughout the world, the response to men and women who are suicidal is to house them in a cell with nothing in it, a 'dry cell', and to place them under constant surveillance. Blanche Hampton describes how 'incidents of self-harm', as they are referred to, are often more common in women's prisons:

> *There is some debate as to whether the current avalanche of self-harm ...*

is a result of general overcrowding, poor conditions, lack of contact with family, the presence of excessive amounts of illegal drugs with dangerous withdrawal effects, sex for favours [where women in desperation for a phone call or drugs can find themselves trading their bodies with unprofessional or predatory male officers], or some hideous combination of them all. (Hampton 1994, p.45)

Stories of survival

Alex Brown [not his real name] was nineteen when I knew him and was on remand on stolen car charges. He wanted to record how he survived, in the hope that it may help others. Over an eight month period Alex was sexually and physically assaulted on what seemed to be endless occasions. Seeking safety, he moved in and out of 'Protection' - an area of the prison within which prisoners can choose to be placed if they feel at risk. Safety cannot be guaranteed within such units, however, and they are often just as dangerous. Alex was repeatedly assaulted both within and outside of 'Protection'. Finally, two older prisoners reached out to him and took him under their wing. When his trial date finally came up he received a non-custodial sentence. Somehow through it all he found the will to stay alive. He held on to his connections with those outside and with his own histories of strength:

I've been strong about it. I've tried to be strong. It's been very hard. I thought there must be something wrong with me if they wanted to do it to me. Why aren't I strong? Why aren't I big? It's taught me how to be a little bit more stronger. I've never really had that much strength emotionally. It was either kill myself or survive. With what I've got outside now I didn't want to ruin my life. I didn't want them to get the satisfaction. They would have thought, 'Ha, he's killed himself because of what we've done'. They'd be boasting about it.

My ex-girlfriend always talked me through situations. She'd say, 'Just be strong and I'll be with you all the way'. When she'd get in trouble at school and she'd have to go to the principal I'd go too: 'Anything you can say to her, you can say to me'. I was really angry at him. I said, 'It's as much my fault as hers'. I guess there was some strength there. That's where I got some of it from. She'd be surprised at what has happened but she wouldn't be surprised at my strength. It's gotten me through this far. Three months ago I was going to kill myself and instead of doing that I've come all this way.

It's come just from myself I guess too. I'm adopted and I've been very strong about that. I've got in trouble before and been strong about that. I have a history of struggling against things. Back then there was no-one to help me out, I had to do it all by myself. My brother was always pleased to see me, never too busy. He'd always be there. If he knew of the strength that I've shown it might give him even more strength. I share everything with him. One day he'll find out about this. It might be next week, it might be next year. I used his spirit to get through. If he was here we'd just talk about it. It'd be very informal. He'd just be here. Hearing his voice would give me strength. I think of the things we have done together.

I brought the spirits of my girlfriend, my ex-girlfriend, my family, my brother, I brought their spirits with me. I thought of the good things in life, what I'd always done that's good and made me happy, a TAFE course I finished. I thought of what I'd do when I got out. I wrote letters to a lot of people. I didn't tell them what happened. I just said, 'I'm feeling a little bit down emotionally - can you write to me and make me feel a little bit better?' On the inside getting a letter is something big.

Some of them say: 'Just fight them off, you know. Just fight the people and everything will be all right'. It's not as easy as that. The whole jail system is not as easy as that. You've just got to put up with it and not do too much. Stand up and you get knocked back down. Just stay down and then find that strength from somewhere. I hope this is of some help to others. (in conversation 1995)

Stories of how women and men have survived the total institution that is prison are largely silenced in this culture. There is little room to consider the ways in which people who have served time and survived have tapped into stories of strength, of connection, of love, rebellion, resistance.

Responses to prison life

I'm locked in here because of my behaviour. My behaviour was not as reprehensible as that being meted out to me. Society condemns my behaviour but accepts the way I am treated. I don't understand this difference in standards and I can't accept it. I don't accept society's views on the treatment of inmates as I am experiencing it. I can't see how it improves anything as what remorse I may have felt has long since been replaced with anger and cynicism. I watch the media deliver news on 'crime' and know it to be false, I hear the evidence against me in court and know it to be false, I see the reports written about me and know them to be false, I mouth the words required about my desire to rehabilitate and nearly choke, but not quite. There is only one game in town, getting out of this place. After that you can all go to hell, with your fantasy legal system, your fantasy penal system, and your fantasy society. (Hampton, 1993, p.146)

As Blanche Hampton describes, living within a prison environment often brings rage. Within an institution designed to punish and humiliate, such justifiable outrage without witness or acknowledgement can at times be turned inwards. The prison context constantly demands that those inside define themselves as 'criminal', as 'bad': *Every time you want something, every aspiration, every lack in your prison life, is blamed on the person that you are, everyday* (Blanche Hampton, in conversation 1996). Those locked within their walls are encouraged to punish themselves:

It encourages people to hate society. I don't know how someone can feel good about themselves when they are so full of hate of society. We punish ourselves. Cutting ourselves up, punching the wall, or by refusing all visits. We cut off all contact with family and friends. Or you go out and abuse a screw knowing you'll be put in segro. Or going off at another inmate knowing they'll get back at you. And that you'll deserve it. I know a guy who refused to have anything in his cell. He went through 18 years without having anything in his cell because he thought he deserved it. The most common way guys punish themselves is that they come in straight as anything and leave as junkies. (Steve Morgan, in conversation, 1995)

Witnessing injustice

I can tell you one significant way that the prison system 'got' me. When I was in prison I saw things done to people that were wrong. I saw injustice. Before prison I was a person who had power over many aspects of my life, not total power but I controlled how I lived my life. If I saw things I didn't like, I would do something about it. In jail, when I saw injustice I found myself doing something really terrible which shames me deeply. If I saw someone resisting and being hurt for it, I would wish for them to stop resisting. I would wish for them to shut up, to lie down and let the beating or other abuse be over and done with, so I wouldn't have to watch it any more, so I wouldn't have to know about it any more. And that little piece of resistance may have been the last little bit that was separating that person from being totally ground down, and I was wishing that they lose even that because being a helpless witness to it caused me such enormous discomfort. (Blanche Hampton, in conversation, 1996)

Shutting down

The worst thing a place can do to you is to take away your emotions. This place did that to me once. I first came to jail as a 21-year-old kid. When I first saw someone get belted I used to really feel for them and wanted to help them. But eventually I could see someone get stabbed and killed and walk over them and feel nothing. I looked out of a window over the circle and everyone looked like fucking robots to me. I had no emotion whatsoever left in me. I didn't feel anything for them. I looked in the mirror and didn't like what I saw. In order to like what I saw I had to do a lot of things.

A lot of guys don't like what they see. That's why so many people commit acts of violence against themselves. It's not always an attempt of suicide. I carry countless scars on me through going through that shit, coming to terms with the fact that I wasn't happy with where my life was going. (Steve Morgan, in conversation, 1995)

Resisting and changing

You need to recognise the fact that if you ever want inner peace in your life you have to change. You can't change what you've done but you can ensure that it doesn't happen again. The biggest factor for change has been the closeness of another person - an officer, professional staff, nurses. In my case it's been a couple of nurses who have made the difference. Somebody gives them a go, somebody believes in them, sees their good side and it's really an emotion thing when you know there are all the people pissed off at you, angry at you, but there's a really beautiful person who sees some goodness in you. Most people in prison have to do it on their own. (Steve Morgan, in conversation, 1995)

Despite the prison context, many of those incarcerated attempt to turn their lives around, to face their histories and harm they may have caused others, in order to move forwards. At the same time, just as prison experiences claim lives and haunt the spirit, some people within prison become stronger through sheer anger and a will to survive:

One thing prison's taught me is to be very strong, and that I am a worthwhile person. Nobody likes to have their freedom taken away from them, but all the abuse and everything they threw at me - it just made me stronger each time. (Padel and Stevenson, in Faith 1993, p.153)

Isolation

Within the US, prisoners who continue to rally against the system are placed within 'control units' where isolation is perfected as a method of control (see Elijah 1995). These units were first developed in the 1960s as a response to increasing numbers of civil rights and anti-war activists being imprisoned and politicising the prison population. In almost every state of the USA a control unit prison now exists. They house those who have committed violence within the system, as well as those who have spoken out, agitated, organised strikes, conducted other political activity behind prison walls, and those who are themselves political prisoners of the USA - those on charges of seditious conspiracy, including Puerto Rican nationalists. Within 'control units', prisoners spend 23 hours of the day in a cell in which the light is always on. Microphones in the cells monitor every sound that each individual makes in the concrete cube. Movement from the cells occurs in shackles.

I was shown around one of these control units. It was there that I saw young men dressed only in white shorts, tattoos upon their back, staring vacantly through the narrow slit called a window. It was there that I felt a tremendous weight upon my being, surrounded by reinforced concrete and the latest technologies of control. In every cell I knew there would be men and women writing writs, and trying to get to speak to us - outsider witnesses. As I walked through, the faces of four women peered out through the perspex. Somehow these women found the strength and generosity of spirit to smile through their cell doors and share a joke with me. Even within such sterile, soulless places, voices of resistance flow.

During the only hour that prisoners are not in their cells, they are encased, still alone, in the 'exercise yard', a room smaller than a bathroom and with less natural light. Separated from others by 25 metres and thick perspex, somehow, through signs, symbols, grunts and shouts across the unit, they communicate with each other. A language of resistance is created and re-created. Somehow, eight scantily dressed men in 'exercise yards', who have never spoken with each other face to face, manage to overcome, temporarily, the design of the $38 million dollar technological isolation unit. Within such bunkers resistance becomes an art in survival.

The art of prison survival

Surviving in the under-world of prisons is just that: an art in survival ... The way of woman's compassion, the cultivation of her complete field of communication, be it eye contact, body language, hand gestures, fragrance, gait, style, through listening to the breathing of the heart, the caress of a soft word - all of this is negated inside the walls of confinement. Commands are barked across lines between them and us. If you can't learn to shut down, you will not survive ... In this world of decay and corruption, we find beauty where we can and we make beauty to live.

Nearly every night we hear muffled crying and almost as often a shrill scream from a nightmare or the strangely quiet slashing of flesh while another throws up. The experience of being locked up with many women, of women strutting proudly in the worst of men's personae, is outlandish. One response is that of women's art.

The creative spirit within the woman's heart is the dominant path to survival ... With the most basic of tools, we fashion beauty and in that beauty, we are empowered and our woman-spirits survive ... (Horii 1994, pp.6-7)

Art is one of many ways in which those imprisoned resist the dehumanising effects of prisons and seek to create ways of living and relating that sustain them and their families through their sentences. The most beautiful murals adorn so many prisons. In San Quentin, California, two huge murals created with kerosene and charcoal were pointed out to me as I walked through the dining area. Prisoners watched our faces as we realised that the trains, aeroplanes and trams depicted on the walls turned as we walked, to face us wherever we stood. In the gallery of a New South Wales prison, creations of beauty are sold: pottery, paintings, carvings. Out of the grey somehow flows such spirit.

Friendships/relationships inside

Maddy: *We kept each other sane.*
Nat: *Total trust. Stripped of everything else, no money, nothing that's yours, nowhere to go but each other ... We spent nearly every minute together or within eyesight everyday from 7am till 10pm when they locked my cell, then we would speak for hours through the 6" by 12" trapdoor.* (Somebody's Daughter Theatre Company 1994, p.32)

Many women and men who have been incarcerated speak of the importance of the relationships of support that they built during their time inside. For women prisoners the relationships of care are perhaps more obvious. For men in prison the little offerings of support mean a lot: 'talking to each other', 'stopping people going off at an officer', 'giving someone else a phone call', 'going two out [sharing a cell] with someone that's decent', 'sharing cigarettes', and 'keeping people's hopes up', are all examples of daily support and resistance.

Sometimes these relationships of support involve a sharing of intimacy as Peter Outlook, a gay man in prison, describes:

Men in prison do have gentle loving sex. You are talking about men who've been locked up for years and are very lonely people. They've been so hard and cold and horrible and nasty that to find someone that they can be intimate with and be emotional with is good for them ... guys in gaol in relationships are intimate and tender. Not much is said, it's all quiet and intimate. Lots of guys won't admit it but it's something special to them. It's something that they wouldn't get to experience out in the real world if they were out there. They've only been able to experience it in gaol.

There are heaps of people that are emotionally dependent on other people in gaol, stacks of them. If you get attached to someone you go through a period when you think, 'Fuck what am I doing?' You start pushing them away: 'Leave me alone', 'Don't touch me'. It's just strange. You turn on each other: 'You're just playing games', 'You're just using me'. There's absolutely no trust, and without trust there's no relationship ... That's why 98% of relationships in gaol fail. You go through periods of no trust and you smash the cell and chop into your cell mate. You end up sitting there cut up on the floor - bleeding, punched and beaten up - both of youse. And it's just like, 'What are we doing?' It goes on all the time. Then you give each other a hug and kiss. It just releases all the anger and frustration out of the view of everyone else.

Jealousy is the worst nightmare. When people see a relationship they just turn green. They go out of their way to take it away from you if they can't have it too. People interfere. They say things that aren't true. Betrayal is so brilliant. People who are my partner's friends are coming on to me left, right and centre. But we made a pact that we'd build trust first, before we did anything, and it worked. We stayed together for three years. (Outlook 1994, pp.16-17)

Release?

Mango: *Then the gate closes. Bang! You're back out there and suddenly you're stuck, even the air's different. I feel sick from the bigness of it all. But I know I can't hang around the entrance of the prison, so I take a deep breath and move, slowly need to move, slowly find my way back, slowly ... BANG! Bad luck love. Signs speeding past, where to go and how fast? Sit on a train, faces staring ... try to act casual but it's a joke because in the end you're different. You can tell by the way people look at you when you've got to report in as an, 'EX Prisoner'. A voice, your voice tells you, 'they think you're worthless." That's the truth. It's me. It's me I hate. It's me I've always hated, and how do you run from yourself? You can't. What's a sure bet to ease the pain?*

Lee: *(Speaks for everyone) Dope.*

(Somebody's Daughter Theatre Company 1994, p.44)

For those women and men who make it out, the effects of imprisonment are often carried long after they walk from prison gates as Blanche Hampton describes:[6]

Within prison you can't appear to be experiencing extremes of any kind because that will count against you. So you develop a kind of pseudo-neutrality and that's what you leave prison with. People then wonder why you're a bit cold! Why you don't react to things any more. I have very delayed reactions to things. Sometimes it's 24 hours before I have a reaction. It's a skilful way of coping with prison life, but once you get out ... The things that you develop to survive in there become the things that stop you from surviving outside.

Of the twelve women I was on remand with, there are only four alive today. They all died outside jail, not inside, but they all died because of jail, or the law, in one way or another. The deaths were connected to either the illegality of drugs and the ramifications of that, or to their becoming completely dysfunctional because of their time in prison and not knowing how to handle things. Death post release seems to be the biggest issue, but it seems to have become invisible to the community and no-one keeps figures on it. I believe it should become visible.

In a pre-release program I was co-facilitating, time after time I would hear that one of the key reasons why people had returned to prison was that 'One of the hardest things out there is that you feel like a nobody. No one says hello. There were all grumpy faces. In here everybody knows my name, says "G'day". Outside nobody even notices'. These statements speak of the lack of community in people's lives in our culture. They also speak of the strength, resourcefulness, humour and intelligence of those in prison, that even within these institutions they can create some sort of community, some sort of home.

Death row

For some prisoners there is no hope of release, of breathing air outside of prison walls again. Somewhere between 10,000 and 16,000 individuals have met their deaths through 'legal' executions during the history of the United States (Wall 1992, p.299). In preparation for this publication I have read pages of detailed descriptions of executions, of innocent and guilty people's last testimonies. I have stood staring into the cell where the condemned spends his or her last night. It is so small, with video camera constant surveillance. Nobody wants to be the person to inject the three different drugs it takes to execute someone in the room I peered into, with its viewing window and its execution slab. In fact they are trying to develop a machine to do it. But someone always has to turn the machine on. As I stood there, I heard of a story of how a man managed to overdose on the morning of his execution. He was resuscitated, his stomach pumped, and then he was killed.

So easily these stories can become words on a page. If I allow myself to truly step into the experiences of these people, to imagine what those final steps must be like, or the years preceding, if I think at any length of the effects witnessing these killings must have on those employed to carry them out, I am overcome with sadness. What I do know is that many of the most callous and brutal prison officials in the US do not believe in the death penalty. For they have met and worked alongside the people that they are then asked to kill, and it is not what they wish to do.

Somehow, and I'm not sure how it can be done, the devastation of state killings must be spoken of, and written about, in ways that don't simply traumatise or sensationalise. My mind flashes an image of the cells of the condemned. I was not allowed to speak to the occupants. They were not allowed to speak to me.

Notes:

1 Blanche Hampton is the author of two books *Prisons and Women* (1993), *and No Escape: Prisons, Therapy and Politics* (1994) based upon her, and other women's, prison experience.

2 A pseudonym name is used here to preserve confidentiality.

3 In June 1982 Mumia Abu-Jamal was sentenced to death for the murder of a white police officer. At the time of his arrest he was a leading African American broadcast journalist in Philadelphia known as 'the voice of the voiceless'. He was also the President of the Philadelphia Association of Black Journalists. His journalism has not ceased since he has been on death row. Proclaiming his innocence and writing passionately and incisively on racism and political bias in the US judicial system, he has become a significant figure in relation to issues of prison and social justice in the US. In mid-1995 Mumia's death warrant was signed, sparking widespread protests throughout the USA. Readings from his book *Live From Death Row* occurred across the country and indeed across the English speaking world. His execution was postponed due to enormous public pressure, but his death warrant could be re-signed at any time.

4 These passages are extracts from *Treat Us Like Queens*, a collection of quotes from groups run with transgender prisoners in the Reception and Induction Centre, Long Bay, New South Wales, in 1995. Soon to be published by the New South Wales Department of Corrective Services.

5 These estimates do not include juvenile centres.

6 These are extracts from an interview which took place with Blanche Hampton in early 1996 in Coogee, New South Wales. Further extracts of the interview are included in chapter 10.

2

Political resistance

I'm 36 years old and have been in jail for 17 years all up, with ten years in child welfare institutions before that. When I first came into the system there was a group of officers who would go from jail to jail to act as the reception committee. They came into my cell after 7:30pm: "Get up against the back wall - cell search." Four screws put me up against the wall and said, 'Reach for the black dot'. But there was no black dot. He hit me with the baton in the kidney. 'Reach for the fuckin' black dot'. I reached until it hurt my calfs. Then he hit me on the back of the head and I just saw red. There was no dot and they were going to keep going. I turned and kicked him in the balls. I got dragged from one wing to another by the hair, bashed and kicked all the way. They threw me in the pound for four days and flogged me each night. On the fifth day I saw a doctor and got eighteen stitches, one arm in plaster, and two broken ribs. (Steve Morgan, in conversation, 1995)

Historically within prisons, relationships of solidarity, defined politically against the system and the prison officers, have been a key avenue for prisoners to claim identity, and a voice. Prison riots, demonstrations and other forms of resistance have been an intricate part of the prison experience. Twenty years ago it was a routine event within Australian prisons for inmates to be physically bashed by prison officers (Royal Commission into New South Wales Prisons 1978). Prisoners were not allowed to look officers in the eye, had to salute regularly, and ensure that the corners of their sheets, blankets, clothing were perfectly straight, or risk unpredictable bashings. The memories are very much alive:

> *I was very nervous the whole time that I was there. If I heard any lock open in the Wing at an unusual time I used to jump out of bed and get up against the back wall. If I heard one screw shout to another or even if I heard local prisoners upstairs talking I used to get out of bed and walk around the cell in confusion not knowing what to do as I was afraid that I would be accused. I used to wash my cell floor with a wet rag four or five times a day so that there was not a speck of dust that could cause me to get a beating. I used to check my buttons over and over to make sure they were done up and I used to clean my toilet by hand three or four times a day. I lived in fear that I had missed some small thing, and I used to get up at 4.00am to sweep the floor.* (Royal Commission into New South Wales Prisons 1978, p.14)

In response to these bashings and intolerable conditions came riots and organised resistance from prisoners that led to the Royal Commission into New South Wales Prisons. Since the Royal Commission handed down its report in 1978 there have been a great many changes. Regular bashings by officers of prisoners are no longer commonplace. The antagonism between 'screw' and 'crim' is still there but it is no longer the battle front that it once was. Improvements to officer training and recruitment, and changes to prison life, including new programs, more flexible property rules, more activities for prisoners and less violence, have all contributed to a lessening of tension.

Instead of violence between officer and prisoner (or in some cases as well as violence) there are now many changes. In the most 'progressive' of prisons there exist quite different relations between officers and prisoners. In some prisons there are regular meetings between prisoner representatives and jail authorities. In an unpublished letter that circulates throughout the New South Wales prison system, a woman prisoner, using the pseudonym of 'Persephone', describes these meetings:

> *I don't think I've ever mentioned 'wing meetings'. They are a custom here. A type of sadomasochistic ritual convicts perform regularly. The idea is that convicts forward suggestions and requests once a week and at the following meeting they are roundly rejected by the hierarchy. We then submit further requests which will be ritually rejected at the following meetings. When convicts feel totally whipped, beaten and*

reduced to worthless, useless blimps (jellyfish on the shores of life) the meeting is considered a success and we adjourn. I'm seeking the origin and purpose of this ancient rite. It seems to be shrouded in mystery ... One barely adjusts to a new rule and before you can say pernicious, foul or even bastard, they have amended it!

In other prisons, officers have become 'case managers' of particular prisoners. They have access to their files and prisoners are expected to consult with and report on aspects of their lives to their case managers - their jailers. Blanche Hampton speaks powerfully of such a situation:

With case management, in prison, power relations become confused. It's very dangerous stuff. These are the people who sign their classification papers, who have power over their parole, their lives, their futures - total power. And then they say, 'Let me at your insides'. And do you think you've got any spirit left after one of those people has had a good go at you? It really makes me very, very angry. It is just so ill-conceived. (Hampton, in conversation, 1996)

Many prisoners describe how the real effects of these 'humanitarian changes' have been to mystify power relations and disguise injustice.

Undermining prisoner solidarity

In some ways though prison was better back then because it was like a family. Crims were crims and they stood all together like they were brothers. If a crim had something that another crim didn't and he didn't need it he would give it. He wouldn't sell it or hire it - he'd give it ...

You had a bible in your cell and that was it. If there was an issue that needed to be fought then nobody had anything to lose by fighting for it ... The attitude back there was one of solidarity - that the inmates should stand united and take their aggression out on the screws or the system instead of each other. And the officers were the same. It was us against them and them against us. Now it's them against them and us against us.

The most obvious reason why these changes have occurred is because of the drug users in prison. Now 75-80% of the guys in gaol are in for drug related offences. They are not real criminals and they should

not be in gaol. They haven't committed any crime other than to support
their drug habit.

But it's also about the oldest trick in the book - divide and conquer.
Get us fighting amongst ourselves and we're leaving them alone. So an
officer will approach one of the more well known inmates and say, 'Be
careful of that guy over there he's an informer or he's a child molester'.
(Wayne, in Wayne & Cheryl 1996)

The increased and more formalised use of prison informers has eroded solidarity according to some prisoners. Those in prison, to some extent, are now policed by other inmates and must always be careful about who they trust in case they are 'dogs' (informers). At the same time a dramatic change has occurred in the prison population with many prisoners now in on drug-related crimes. As Wayne described above, there is a perception that drugs and drug culture have eroded trust.

Maintaining control and order within prisons is a primary aim of prison officials. Often this involves breaking down prisoner solidarity and the use of 'behaviour management strategies'. In US prisons, Dr. Edgar Schein has played an important role. Dr Schein studied Chinese 're-education' of US POWs during the Korean War and then elaborated upon its application to US prisons in a conference with representatives from the Bureau of Prisons in 1962. There he spoke of the use of brainwashing, sensory deprivation, and perceptual deprivation, in order to deal with prisoners who resist the system.

His work was built upon by Dr James McConnell who, in 1970, delivered an article entitled 'Criminals can be brainwashed now'. The implementation of these ideas has included the use of drugs, restraints, long-term solitary confinement and even psychosurgery (Ryan 1995). The current control units, described in chapter 1, seem to be the latest institutional development of their ideas. Dr Schein, back in 1961, provided the Bureau of Prisons with a list of specific methods of control, all of which are commonplace in today's prisons:

1. *Physical removal of prisoners to isolated areas to effectively break*
    and seriously weaken close emotional ties.
2. *Segregation for all natural leaders.*
3. *Use co-operative prisoners as leaders.*
4. *Prohibit group activities not in line with brainwashing objectives.*
5. *Spy on prisoners and report back private material.*
6. *Trick men to write statements which are then shown to others.*

7. *Exploitation of opportunists and informers.*
8. *Convince the prisoners they can trust no-one.*
9. *Treat those willing to collaborate in far more lenient ways than those not willing.*
10. *Punish those who show unco-operative attitudes.*
11. *Systematically withhold mail.*
12. *Prevent contact with anyone non-sympathetic to the treatment and regimentation of the captive populace.*
13. *Hold a group to ridicule consisting of prisoners abandoned by and totally isolated from the social order.*
14. *Disorganise all group standards among prisoners.*
15. *Undermine all emotional supports.*
16. *Prevent prisoners from writing home to family and friends in the community describing conditions of their confinement ... Place individuals in new, ambiguous situations where standards are deliberately kept unclear; then, apply pressure to conform to desired orders to win favours and reprieves from the pressure ...*

(Shakur et al. 1995, pp.64-65)

With solidarity eroded, prison conflicts, rather than politicising prison conditions or the make-up of the prison population, now commonly involve racial conflict or conflict between those prisoners in the main and those in 'Protection' who are suspected of being informants. Violence between prisoners is not new, however many older prisoners declare that they preferred it how it used to be. Despite the bashings, the strict routines, the riots, and fewer 'privileges', they state, just as Wayne described above, that there was once a sense of solidarity, identity, and an avenue for resistance and that this made all the difference. Whatever the case, there is often articulated a longing for solidarity to protest the current realities of prison life.

Indigenous Australian solidarity

When I first came to gaol I had relations here. The Kooris have all got a bond. White fellas ain't got that. Everyone's there for each other. Because of that, Kooris have more power in gaol than on the outside and some Kooris get more respect in prison than when they're out. (Billy, Fred and Eddie 1994, p.14)

In contrast to the overall erosion of prisoner solidarity, today, within Australian prisons, there is a growing momentum of political resistance. Indigenous Australians are actively involved in political struggle. Campaigning on issues of deaths in custody and imprisonment rates, reconnecting with cultural practices, and naming past and present injustices, are daily acts of political struggle taking place behind prison walls. This action and the ripples from it offer enormous hope in relation to the possibilities for change. For Indigenous Australians within prisons, solidarity has in many ways been maintained:

There's support with the Kooris. As soon as I came in it was like I'd known them for years. They took me in, talking about family, different things, what-not. In the outcome we were all sort of related. We've left our family outside so this is our family in here. We stand by each other whatever the cost. (Billy, Fred and Eddie 1994, p.14)

3

The families of
prisoners

The effects of prison touch many lives. Sharon Gollan, a Ngarrindjeri[1] woman who was involved in the Reclaiming Our Stories, Reclaiming Our Lives project,[2] describes her experience of visiting her brother in prison:[3]

I can see this picture of the very first time I visited my brother when he went to prison. He was very young. He'd just turned 18. Before going in, I remember my sister and my other brother saying to me: 'Don't show him that you're upset. Don't show him that. Don't cry. Be strong.' I remember him walking through the door. To me he was still like a baby brother, and he was also like a son, so of course it was hard not to connect into the sadness of seeing him there. I was also worried about him, because he was so young. I was thinking, 'My goodness, how's he going to cope? and all this sort of stuff. It was really hard but I knew that in the end I had to be really strong for him, because I didn't want him to then be worried about me.

He came over and he was watching my face really closely, so I made myself be strong right at that moment and not want to cry. And so we were being noticeably very loud and not actually talking about what we really wanted to talk about. Just before we were leaving we talked about taking care - taking care of yourself. He actually grew a beard, and to me that was a sign that he was telling me that he would be all right, because the beard made him look older.

My sister, who's younger than me, was also teaching me these sorts of things: 'He has to do this now'. So not through so many words, but through our talking, through our eyes, and really not talking out loud, we were saying a lot about taking care of yourself in prison and we'll be all right out here.

Thinking about my brother, there's been a lot of death. He has to deal with a lot physically and emotionally away from us. There's always been the silencing. But also the words that go through to say: 'You're with us. When it's your birthday, you're acknowledged. At times of grieving you're acknowledged and you're here.'

Despite all the restraints and the debilitating effects of imprisonment upon families, ways to communicate love and support across prison lines are found. Men and women in prison are often sustained by their connections with the outside world. Time inside is structured around phone calls and visits.

The consequences of imprisonment on the partners and families of those imprisoned are often forgotten. For every man imprisoned, and for every woman, other people are affected. It is overwhelmingly mothers, girlfriends, and wives who visit prisons, who undergo strip-searches, long trips, degrading comments and the sadness involved in supporting loved ones through terms of imprisonment. It is overwhelmingly women who look after the children after one or both parents are incarcerated, usually while working and attempting to send money into the prisons to make life inside a little easier.

Many men in prison state that they believe that their partners 'do the time' harder than they do. They have all the added responsibilities and at the same time many experience discrimination from neighbours, relatives, parents of their children's friends. They become 'criminal' by association. The children of prisoners live with their own experiences of visits, of discrimination, of parents behind bars and in uniform. The partners, family and children of prisoners report that to be forced to turn their faces away when visiting-time is over, to hear the gates close behind them with their loved one locked inside, can be an ordeal.

When those who survive prison are released, often brutalised by the experience, if they have anywhere to turn it is usually to mothers, lovers and sisters - who are left to cope with the ongoing consequences of their incarceration. Imprisonment affects so many lives in ways that go unnoticed and unnamed.

Deaths in custody

Many people's sons, daughters, sisters and brothers do not return home. With deaths in custody occurring at alarming rates, the families of those in prison live with a constant fear. Deaths in custody leave families and communities not only grieving, but with a sense of deep powerlessness, with uncertainty, and the impossibility of ever knowing exactly what happened to those they loved. The death of a loved one is in itself a profoundly sad experience. When a death occurs within a prison, isolated, and often violently, the feelings of shame, guilt, anger and powerlessness can be overwhelming.

As described in the Reclaiming Our Stories, Reclaiming Our Lives project, for Indigenous Australian families and communities, deaths in custody have additional meaning, outrage and grief as they occur in white institutions, with devastating regularity and in the context of the effects of genocidal practices. Ray Jackson, the chairperson of the New South Wales Aboriginal Deaths in Custody Watch Committee, describes how deaths of Aboriginal people in prison are not considered as suicide by Indigenous Australian communities:

The whole idea of locking people up is alien, totally alien to our people. But that is not the reason why our people are killing themselves. Our people have been put in jail for over 200 years. And you take the early Kooris, they were basically locked up from the age of ten. So there's nothing about a jail that is strange or anything like that. The reason that Aboriginal people die in custody is very simple. Jail is the most unnatural environment on this planet. When you get young people of 21, 22 years old and it's their first time in prison, with the fear of rape, bashings, the standover which goes on everyday in jails, some of them can't handle it and they break and they hang themselves. But we don't call that suicide. We don't call it suicide.

The voices of families and communities that are affected by imprisonment are often silenced. Their stories of survival and struggle speak of the ways in which the effects of prisons and imprisonment ripple outwards throughout the culture.

Notes

1. One of the traditional Indigenous clan groups in South Australia.

2   See *Dulwich Centre Newsletter*, 1995, No.1.

3   This interview took place at Dulwich Centre, Adelaide, South Australia, in early 1996. Further extracts are included in chapter 11.

4

Working
behind bars

Workers who choose to make a career within prisons often spend more time behind the razor wire than most prisoners. Such an experience can drastically affect one's life outside. It is easy to become captivated by the prison world and find it impossible to convey its realities to those to whom one is close. It is easy to be overcome by the brutality or to have to shut down to the experience of others. Some workers are affected by the sense of powerlessness. Others go to great lengths to find warmth and connectedness within prison walls to compensate in some way for its coldness. For women workers, the sexual politics within ultra-masculine institutions is an added dimension.

For whatever reason, workers within prison are often forever changed by their time inside. This was certainly the case for me. My experiences of working within prisons, and that of other non-custodial workers, will be considered in later chapters. The following pages seek to explore the experiences of custodial officers.

Custodial culture

> *I do not forget ... the good guards, polite, just and human - a corner of blue sky in this penitentiary hell.* (Hampton 1993, p.143)

It is easy for those critical of the prison system to ignore the experiences of prison officers. What is it like for them to find themselves locking people up and at times playing a part within brutal and degrading prison cultures? The stories that prison officers have to tell may prove crucial if we are to move beyond prisons. Prison officers are often young working-class men (although numbers of women officers are increasing), or ex-members of the military, who guard people who are from communities like their own. They find themselves working within an ultra-masculine military culture, with strict ranking and chains of command. They are squeezed between supervising and guarding prisoners, while at the same time being under surveillance themselves by internal investigation units and their superiors.

Trevor Pugh spent seven years working as a prison officer within South Australian prisons. He spoke with me in July 1996 in Adelaide:

I grew up working-class in Victoria. My father was a labourer. Well he was a printer first off - a qualified printer - but he didn't enjoy the indoors. And for years he was a milkman with a horse and cart, which I ended up doing as well. We met many people through the dairies and through dealing with horses, so that was quite interesting. And of course I started to meet a lot of people that were on the other side of the law. I used to go down the pub with Dad from a young age, just to be with him. We spent a lot of time together that way and I saw how different jobs affected different people.

At one of the pubs we drank at, there were bricklayers, builders, architects - all the range of building trades. They all stuck in their own little groups. Quite often, if a fight started in one area, the others sort of just moved back and let that group fight their own fight and that was it - they weren't going to get involved with people. I thought it was a terrible way to be - not concerned about another person - but I grew up with the attitude that you minded your own business because everyone's got their own problems. I wasn't in a position to help.

Education was just technical school and then it was out into the real world working. I learnt all my experience in the streets and working. I never had trouble getting a job because there was plenty of jobs around in those days. Quite a few of my mates had been inside. I used to be laughed at because I'd never done any time. I thought, 'Well, I'm not stupid enough to get caught.' I got plenty of clips over the ears by the cops, or a boot up the arse. You know, drink-driving, just being 'a lad' as they called them in those days. That was just part and parcel of growing up. But when I got to around twenty-two, I'd been drinking since I was fifteen, I was injured when I was doing the milk-round. I decided that I could have been killed at any time so I decided to live up life. I think in a matter of a year I got thrown in jail for drunk and disorderly and fighting probably six or seven times because I wanted to be accepted by the others. I could come out and say, 'Yeah, I copped a kicking by the cops in there because I was giving them cheek', things like that, and I was just lucky that there were no convictions. They were a lot more lenient in those days.

But I realised where it was going to head. I was getting older and a lot of guys were getting into light-scale larceny and were heading up the scale. When I was about twenty-three, I decided the best way was to leave the area. I came over to South Australia with my partner at the time. I broke out of that circle of people that would have taken me down. Most of them are now dead, whether it has been through drugs, motorbike or car accidents. That was their lifestyle - live hard and fast. We moved to South Australia. It wasn't until I came over here that my interest in life came back. After we separated I came back down to live in the city and that's where the opportunity came to become a Correctional Officer.

I'd always been interested in helping people, but I never had the chance to do higher education, as in social work or anything like that. I felt Corrections was the way to go - working with people in a prison. I was thirty years old. I believed that I'd had the experience by that time to possibly make a difference, because theory is great, but practical experience counts. I was in for a hell of a shock when I got in there.

It was totally different to what I had expected. I found out, much to my disbelief, that there wasn't the rehabilitation, there wasn't the care I expected. You didn't get involved. Actually if you took too much time with a prisoner that was having problems you were called a social worker by the fellow officers and told to just do your job and leave that to the 'do-gooders', so to speak. You were caught in a sort of a situation where sometimes you desperately wanted to help someone and other times where you had to bow to peer pressure. The prisoners were in the same way. But it was a steady job. It was a challenge, and I did manage to help some people. I thought for every person I can help, that made it worthwhile but there wasn't enough opportunity - they were sort of exceptions rather than the rule.

Officers are living on the edge all the time and the only way they can cope is the same way as the prisoners: put on that vicious face and be aggressive. They are virtually trying to scare each other. That is a cycle in the prison system. They've got nothing else to hold onto, because if they show any weakness it's like a pack of wolves - every one just turns on them. That happens to officers against officers and prisoners against prisoners. It's all a big bluff - the whole lot is a big bluff. There are a lot of officers who start out as caring. They're not all violent but they become immune to the violence because of what's around them and it just rubs off on them. They take it home. And then when they have trouble at home they release it at work in different ways, through petty little things which annoy the prisoners. This then makes them angry and it's a vicious circle.

Officers are dealing with it through alcohol, or their marriages are breaking up. After years in the job, you become like the people you are guarding. You become like the prisoners in respect of - you've got to be tough, you can't show fear. You will find that with any long-term serving officer (which is normally over, say, five years) they become hard, cynical - very cynical. They will laugh after they deal with someone that has slashed up or overdosed, because that's the way to deal with it. If you let it get to you, it gets to you very badly and you can't function.

A lot of officers will get involved in fights out in the street. They don't give anyone a second chance out there - because they've got to give too many second chances in prison, and so they become quite violent. I know that feeling. I swore when I first got out of the prison service that if anyone threatened me in any way, I would just flatten them, no questions asked. I totally believed that I would do that and I had the opportunity with a good friend who had insulted my wife. But fortunately at the time I found common sense. I had been out long enough.

Working in a prison if you show any sort of weakness the other officers then stay clear of you, and you have to prove yourself again. That happened to me. I had been in the job for about two and a half or three years and I got on okay with officers and prisoners. But then at the Remand Centre I thought I had been infected with AIDS from a prisoner. I'd done the right thing. He'd been taken down to the infirmary and he had none of his gear, so a couple of the other prisoners - knowing myself - they asked if I could take his gear down to him. Otherwise by the time they had got someone else to do it, it could be two or three days. So I packed up his gear and in the process I thought I had become infected. I had to undergo blood tests for quite a while.

It affected my home life, because of the fear of contracting AIDS or HIV. I didn't have any contact with my daughters for a long time because I was concerned I could transfer it to them. I can understand what a prisoner feels like when they could be infected or they believe they are, it can be soul destroying. Dying never worried me. I think most officers are, if they're going to get bashed up then they're going to get bashed up, if you're gonna get killed, you're gonna get killed. That's part and parcel of being in the job. If you are scared of that you shouldn't be in the job. But the virus was different. HIV - if you get full-blown - is a wasting disease, and I didn't want to go that way because I'd seen a lot of other prisoners go that way.

I didn't have help, even though I was on the outside, because the Department wasn't interested. I got compensation payments, as in stress leave. Finally, after about six blood tests, I found that I was clear. I had to convince myself to get back into living, instead of wasting away, because that's what was happening. It was affecting me mentally and physically. When I went back to the Remand Centre I found out that I had become claustrophobic possibly because of the lack of air and the fear of getting another infection.

I ended up transferring up to another prison which had a campus-style living area, and started back on track again. But I felt that up there the officers were, if anything, more detached than I had ever been - even when I was crook. They were in there getting paid and that's all they wanted. They didn't really care about the people. They were just interested in the money and that's it. And to me, if you're in a job which you don't enjoy you're in the wrong job. I had to prove myself to the officers there that the reason I had been out on stress was not because I was scared of prisoners, which meant I had to be honest. It's amazing how much doubt they have of you if you can't survive in a prison system, even with the officers. They will virtually force you out of a job.

I caused waves. I came to logger-heads with a lot of them because of the way I treated people. I would stop in the evening when we were locking them up; if a prisoner was upset (which you found quite often) I would stop and talk to them, if they wanted to talk. When you know a prisoner is going through bad times and you care, you'll write reports or tell someone about it. Now quite often people on the next shift didn't care - they'd be too interested in staying in their office reading a book, having a laugh or whatever with someone else - another officer, and you'd go back to that unit the next day and find that the prisoner had been transferred to the labour prison, or was in hospital because he slashed up - because no-one followed up. That was a heart-breaking part of it, because these people were screaming out for help but the people in there didn't care enough. That used to affect me deeply, plus after the AIDS scare, seeing all the blood if someone had slashed up, that affected me to a certain degree. And visits. It's terrible to be an officer during visits. Visitors actually pull their children away from you. When an innocent child will come up to say 'Hello', they will pull their children away from you, 'Don't speak to him - he's a screw'.

I became involved in 'the squad' [a unit of officers called in to quell disturbances and 'secure' prisoners]. *Not for the express purpose of what a lot of officers joined it for - to bash prisoners when they got the chance - but to be there to help officers that were in trouble and to secure prisoners if they were playing up. The quicker you could subdue them, by using proper restraint holds which I was used to in martial arts, the easier it was on them - people didn't have to resort to violence. And I can say that while I was with prisoners in the squad, no-one got any undue physical force that wasn't necessary. I grew up with that belief that you can't take advantage of someone that is at a disadvantage.*

But because of my 'outspoken' ways I got my elbow busted in squad training by an officer. I never got over that - I was in chronic pain for a long time and I ended up getting out of the Department because of it. I still have the chronic pain today. I was on all manner of pain killers which made no difference and I lost the ability to meditate and take control, which martial arts had helped me learn for many years. It wasn't until I got out of the prison system and possibly a year and a half down the track that I got back the ability to subdue the anger about what had happened to me and actually take control of my life.

You just take a long time to recover from the prison system - even as an officer. I know many officers that have left the job and it takes probably a year - a year and a half - to actually get back to a form of living normally and deal with problems without an initial violent attitude coming out.

I think everyone is responsible to do something. You can cry, you can laugh but I think action and actually speaking out about your feelings will allow others to understand that it is possible. I'd like to believe that officers could speak out without being made a laughing stock but it's a body armour they get up. I'm not lagging or being a dog on anyone. There are a lot of things I could speak about but it would be betraying what some prisoners have told me, how they survive in there. Even though it would be nice to be able to tell others how to survive in there it would give away the game and they wouldn't be able to use that. So there's a fine line about what you can say. And officers are in the same boat. They've all got their little survival tricks whether it be giving prisoners smokes, turning a blind eye to certain things. That's their little tricks that they've developed which makes them believe that they're doing that little thing that makes a difference.

Over all those years I met a lot of fantastic officers. I'd like to say to them - don't just sit there and take it. Say your piece, just let it be known that you don't agree. Don't just sit there and accept what's happening. It might be a job and it might be money but why did you get into the job in the first place? Was it for the reason of helping people? Or was it for a reason of controlling people? Think of why you got in there and think of why you should be in the job and that's about it. Don't be scared of having feelings because if you're not careful you become like the people you're looking after. Look at your own family life and how it affects you. Talk about it.

I've dealt with most things in life through humour and jokes. I always got a quick word in - you know, make light of the situation because if you don't laugh, you cry and sooner or later you're all cried out and you still go nuts. After I left the Department the dream inside of me still was to help people and I realised that once you are in the prison system, there's no real way you can help 'em. The only way is to stop them from getting into the prison system. And so now I'm working on that, with kids, young offenders. We've got to keep them out.

5

Survivors of men's violence:
Experiences of court
and prison

*When I'm hurting and I'm angry, I don't give a damn what happens to
the man who hurt me - I'm emotionally exhausted. But - for me - the
prison system has provided no protection, because he still harasses me.*
(A member of WOWSafe)

WOWSafe, Women of the West for Safe Families, is an organisation
of women in Adelaide, South Australia, who have personally survived men's
violence in the home and now campaign in order to prevent it in the lives of
others. This chapter is based on the ideas, contributions and experiences of the
WOWSafe women which were offered both through writings and consultation.

The previous chapters have provided glimpses of the prison system
and described its effects throughout many people's lives. Most people within
prison are incarcerated for *non*-violent offences. The perception that only
violent men and women are incarcerated perpetuates class and race injustice. As
Part Two of this book goes on to describe, it is far more likely for women and
men to be incarcerated due to the direct and indirect effects of poverty and/or
racism, than it is for them to be incarcerated due to crimes of violence. As
prisons are upheld as this culture's primary response to violence, however, this
chapter seeks to explore the experiences of the survivors of men's violence. It

focuses on two of the most common forms of violence in our culture: sexual assault and domestic violence.

Safety and relief

There were certainly days and nights that I would have jumped for joy to know that he was in custody, simply to know that we could sleep soundly for just one night. (A member of WOWSafe)

The WOWSafe women state that for many people, women and children in particular, far from representing an institution of torture or degradation, prisons have at times been necessary for their safety. When the men who have been violent towards them have been incarcerated, the women have been free from the abuse. As the incarceration of a man who has been violent is often seen as a societal acknowledgement of wrong-doing, and that in some circumstances it offers physical protection, imprisonment can bring enormous relief.

Protection is rare

Most of the violent men are not in jail. Thinking about prisons is pointless for us, for hardly any of them are there. (A member of WOWSafe)

The WOWSafe women describe how actually achieving safety through the police, courts and prison is extremely rare. They point to a number of reasons why this is the case. Firstly, the police can rarely offer meaningful protection as they take thirty to forty minutes to arrive. Secondly, if men dispute restraining orders they nearly always win. And thirdly, if charges are laid, men are often given bail. Even when this is not the case, in order to achieve the safety that a prison sentence sometimes represents, women have to go through court experiences which are often re-traumatising and offer little in terms of achieving a sense of justice.

The courtroom

Pia van de Zandt works for the Department of Women, a New South Wales state government department. She has recently been exploring the experiences of women in court and offered the following written reflections on the project and her involvement in it:[1]

> *I have been working with a team of researchers looking at the experiences of women in court as victims of sexual assault. To do this work we have looked at prosecution files and listened to sound recordings of sentence hearing and trials. The study has looked at every sexual assault matter in the District Court in New South Wales, over a one-year period, which has involved an adult female victim of a recent sexual assault. In doing this we have listened to the victims of sexual assault give evidence and be cross-examined in court. We also collected direct quotes from the judge, lawyers and from the victim in court herself, some of which are interesting, funny, brave and shocking, and most of which are horrifying.*
>
> *The legal system and the adversarial trial which positions her story against his is designed to result in an ultimate finding of truth. The victim of the assault doesn't have her own representative in the courtroom, she is only the 'primary witness or the complainant in the matter'. The Crown Prosecutor calls her to give evidence but is not her advocate. The Prosecutor is the advocate for the State or Crown and prosecutes the charge on behalf of the people of the State. The accused person has his own legal advocate to defend the charges against him on his behalf.*
>
> *Her story or the way she may want to tell her story, or in the case of Aboriginal women, or women from particular cultures, the way she may* need *to tell her story, is irrelevant except when and as it fits into the legal construction of sexual assault. Her experience of the sexual assault is not important - she is only required to give evidence which makes out the elements of the offence - this evidence relates to how many times, what time, how many bruises, how many fingers, how loud was the scream, how many hours later did you tell someone, why didn't you kick him, why did you live with him for two months after, if he hit you why did you stay ...?*
>
> *A victim is often told to tell the court what happened, not how she felt. Defence Counsel: 'Just stick to what happened Ms ... not what you felt'.*
>
> *In the court, the masculine, adversarial, and I would now say deliberately misogynist culture forces women to tell the story of the sexual assault in particular ways. Like the assault itself, it is in the trial, in this experience of being compelled to re-tell their story within rules*

that are made up by a different gender, that they are victimised and abused all over again. I have listened to hearings in which the woman has had to stop 12 times because of her distress or has regurgitated in the witness box due to the pain of re-telling her story in these ways. It's no wonder that women say: 'I would tell others not to bother, because you are worse off at the end of it. I went through all that and nothing came out of it.' 'I felt I was treated badly. I would never go through it again or advise anyone else to go through it.' [2]

Having heard these trials, I believe women are as much victims in court as they are at the time of the sexual assault and that their recovery can really only begin after their trial.

The project has raised a number of dilemmas for me in relation to my participation in the legal system and within the bureaucracy. Having studied law, I am employed as a policy officer looking at legal issues. I am paid to make small critiques of the legal system, to tinker with aspects of the law in a comparatively small way to make it better for women. My job does not normally involve unpacking the institution of the law or exposing it as the oppressive system it can be.

I found it very difficult being a passive researcher. I was hearing stories of women, listening to their oppression, and I was just taking down details, passively, fitting their experiences into a box to be plugged into a machine and spat out as a series of numbers. The numbers were printed out as tables and put into a bureaucratic report which, because of its targetted audience, uses complicated legal language. I have wondered whether I am just rewriting or reconstructing the stories of these women in similar ways as the court reconstructs their stories.

As a bureaucrat I have toned down my writing and my comments are edited. I have put a political gloss on the information. I work with judges, lawyers, and legal policy officers, and am careful not to offend them too much by what I say. I make a choice to work within the bureaucratic machine, and at times I sit with judges and senior bureaucrats discussing possible amendments and legislation, regulations and clauses, not daring to take up the responsibility to challenge the whole system.

I certainly feel differently about the law now and my place in it. I have heard firsthand of the ways in which a system, which is supposed to uphold rights and provide justice, victimises women and many others. How to get the work recognised now, and acted upon, how to be part of that change process, is a next step.

Collusion of the courts

The WOWSafe women describe how not only does the legal system fail to protect many of the survivors of men's violence, and often re-traumatises them in the process, but in many circumstances the courts also serve to inadvertently collude with men in not taking responsibility for their actions:

If a man does want to take some responsibility for his crimes - for example in cases of child sexual assault - if he does feel some regret, some remorse - as soon as they own up they will be found guilty. To be responsible means prison as a consequence. But, if he pleads not guilty, he'll get off nearly every time. The other side of this is that prison gets to be associated with guilt. Men get an attitude of, 'If I was guilty I'd go to jail'. All other forms of taking responsibility get lost along the way. (a member of WOWSafe)

After imprisonment

For those survivors of men's violence who are able to, and choose to, go through with a prosecution, it is relatively rare to end up obtaining a guilty verdict for the man, and fewer still a prison sentence. The WOWSafe women describe the mixture of reactions that can accompany a conviction of the perpetrator and the dilemmas raised in relation to prisons being the response to men's violence:

When a criminal is sent to prison, he is removed from all his societal obligations in relation to the crime for which he was convicted. His sentence represents his obligation - however, there is no longer any connection to the crime. That connection was severed as part of the due process of the law. For many men, jail becomes the responsibility - doing one's time. Their responsibility for what they've actually done is never encouraged. But from a victim's perspective, who continues to shoulder that responsibility? Who is left with debts to pay, children to raise? Who is referred to in the community as 'wife of a crim' rather than survivor of the abuse? GUESS! (a member of WOWSafe)

Guilt

I don't want to feel any more guilt for 'breaking up the family' or for 'ruining the health of my mother-in-law' or for 'the death of my father-in-law'. If you ask any of the people who used to call themselves my friends, they believe I'm guilty.

They know he bashed me, they know he tried numerous times to kill me, they watched while he raped me; they saw it all, and still they believe I deserved it because I married him. I know logically I'm not guilty, but on some deep level I still feel I must have done something terrible that I can't remember. There has to be some reason that he treated me that way. It's difficult to come to terms with those feelings when society still places the emphasis on his guilt rather than my innocence. I consider myself lucky that I wasn't forced to participate in my partner's activities. I know one woman who was and she still carries the guilt totally, as if her partner should never accept responsibility. (a member of WOWSafe)

Ongoing fear of violence

When you try to find out when he is getting parole they say: 'He's done his time. You mustn't keep this going, He's done his time.' I don't want to be the one to fear the day my ex is released from prison. I remember his anger when I left - the persistent stalking, the intimidation, the knowledge of what he could do if he chose. After years, I've found a way to live past all that, and I don't want to return to that half-life. In those days, every move I made was determined by him, in spite of his often physical absence. No more! (a member of WOWSafe)

The WOWSafe women point out that often prisons do not serve to protect the survivors of men's violence. Imprisonment is by no means a 'final solution', as there is often a continued fear of when the perpetrator of violence may be released. As described above, this information is often hard to come by. What's more, the WOWSafe women describe how many women continue to experience harassment from their incarcerated partners. With nearly all of their life out of their control, men's attempts to control and dominate their partners can be escalated by imprisonment. Irregular phone calls and connections with friends outside are often used as forms of surveillance and domination.

Dilemmas

The WOWSafe women describe in detail the dilemmas for them of imprisonment acting as a response to men's violence:

I don't believe prisons serve any purpose. I feel sorry for those who are made to endure them. I suppose all of this doesn't really have to do with prison, but with acceptance of responsibility. My ex and probably many others will probably never accept responsibility for what they've done, no matter what their punishment is. If his imprisonment is the only way for us to be safe, then it should be that way. While I wouldn't treat the most vicious animal like a prison inmate, I have trouble equating my ex-partner with a member of the human race. He treated my children and me with such inhumanity that I picture him as nothing more than an animal. I have trouble caring what society does to him.

Society needs to view the situation without the tunnel vision of 'the law' - passing the buck of responsibility is not good enough. Inventing and examining prison as 'punishment' is a token gesture, speciously presented as a way to protect victims and provide them with retribution. Women are socialised to be nurturing, caring, beautiful human beings; I'm one, and so are most of my friends. There is no way that we should give up that part of ourselves to satisfy society's need for retribution. It can serve no purpose, because what's done cannot be undone. I just want to get on with my life. I just want to be safe from him. I want to live, and die in peace. I want my prison walls to disappear, so that I can enjoy life, but while society still treats me as if I had some control over what he did to me, I will protect myself within these walls because I'm safer there. I don't need to see him in prison to know that he's guilty, but I need some process to show society that I'm not guilty, that he was responsible.

For all the years in my prison, I found a way to survive. One of the things that keeps me going is the realisation that I was stronger than him to survive what he dished out. There exists an inner strength in me that I don't think he possesses. Even so, without society's help, I'll still be in my prison. I need some way to break my walls down, I don't need to have walls built around him. (a member of WOWSafe)

Notes

1   The Department for Women will publish the results of this research in November 1996 titled 'Heroines of Fortitude: The Experiences of Women in Court as Victims of Sexual Assault'. Copies are available from the New South Wales Women's Information and Referral Service.

2   New South Wales Sexual Assault Committee; *Sexual Assault Phone-In Report*, Women's Co-ordination Unit (Now Department for Women), August 1993.

Exploring the Politics of Imprisonment

The aim in Part One of this book has been to offer a glimpse into life within prison and its broader effects. I have tried to describe what I and others have found behind prison gates, a world of dispossession of spirit, a world that creates criminality and violence. I have attempted to sketch some of the ways in which people survive prison, and to show the ways in which the effects of these institutions ripple outwards to families, children, and those who work within them. I have tried to give space for others to voice their experiences of surviving violence, both inside and outside of prison. If reading this book enables people to enter the world of the prison, we can also close the pages, walk out of the prison gates, and hear them shut behind us. But we can also choose whether or not we remember the stories and the songs of survival.

In Part One I have also tried to illustrate how attempts to critique the criminal justice system and imprisonment often raise complicated issues. My aim in Part Two is to explore some of these issues further through an examination of the politics of imprisonment. In it I address the question: 'Just who is it that we imprison, and from which communities do they come?' I explore the relationship between imprisonment and issues of gender, class and culture, and ask why it is that imprisonment has such disproportionate effects on communities of people of colour, working-class communities, and communities of Indigenous Peoples. Identifying gross injustices within the 'justice system', I then seek to investigate how it is that the politics of imprisonment can remain so invisible, and how the professions of psychology and education play their part in contributing to this invisibility. This is then followed by an exploration of notions of punishment and protection. The following questions, amongst others, are addressed: 'Is it desirable and possible to move away from notions of retribution when they so saturate our lives? How can we find ways to talk about the dilemmas regarding imprisonment as a response to men's violence? Can we create the contexts for new conversations and new partnerships that may herald alternative community responses?'

The last chapter in this section returns to issues of class and culture, and explores the more personal politics of imprisonment. But, to begin, the following pages describe how we are in an era of increasing imprisonment, a time in which greater and greater numbers of prisons are being built, and more and more people locked away.

6

The state
of the prison

The USA

The USA currently imprisons more people per head of population than any other country in the western world. There are now over five million citizens of the USA under the control of the criminal justice system, including a record 1.5 million in federal and state prisons and local jails, and 3.5 million convicted criminals on probation and parole. The numbers behind bars or on probation and parole will soon approach six million, equal to the number of full-time students in the nation's four-year colleges (*The San Francisco Chronicle,* Thursday August 10 1995, p.A2). Between 1981 and 1991 the US Federal Government cut its contribution to education by 25% (in real dollars) and increased its allocation to criminal justice by 29% (Prejean 1995, p.9).

Eddie Ellis, who served 23 years within the New York prison system, has now, with others, developed a prisoner education, research and advocacy organisation, which is described in detail in chapter 15. He describes the present situation:

It costs $125,000 to build one prison cell and conservatively $25,000 to keep one person in prison for one year. What are we getting for this sort of money? White middle-class people have to start asking, 'What did we get for the $1,250,000 we spent to lock him up for 10 years. We could have sent him to Harvard for four years instead - we'd save $1,000,000! What's the return?' (in conversation, 1995)

Prison policy in the US is now driven to some extent by economic forces, as Nils Christie describes:

President Dwight Eisenhower, back in the 1950s, warned against the military establishment fuelled by a military industry's need for profits and jobs. Today it's the same with the penal establishment. In California the prison guards' association gives millions to those politicians who are for the expansion of the prison industry, and tries to block those who are opposed. (Christie, in Swift 1996a, p.11)

More and more prisons are being built across the country at an alarming rate. However, there is still gross overcrowding, particularly in local jails. Alternatives to mainstream incarceration are also being tried, including boot-camps or shock-camps in which prisoners, often young offenders, are met with 'devastating' streams of verbal abuse and 'unceasing' bullying, are forbidden to look officers in the eye and, in strict military fashion, obeying every word spoken, participate in rigorous army-like drills and exercises (Polsky & Fast, cited in Atkinson 1995, p.5).

In Arizona, the work-gangs in chains are back on the sides of the roads, and some prisons, to save money (and in the belief that it may deter crime), have been set up in the deserts with accommodation in tents, with only broth and bread for each of the daily meals. Outside prison walls there are over 12,000 offenders in all 50 states of the US now confined within their homes with constant electronic surveillance (Polsky & Fast, cited in Atkinson 1995, p.5).

Recent changes to the law continue the spiral of imprisonment. Mandatory sentences are now in existence for the possession of certain amounts of drugs. 'Three strikes and you're out' laws give inmates with two prior offences a mandatory life sentence for their third. The recent Crime Bill added 50 new offences to those that currently lead to a penalty of death. Across the USA, this very moment, there are twenty-four hundred people living on death row, awaiting execution. Due to recent legislative change, the vast majority of these will no longer be able to appeal their sentences of death.

Australia and Aotearoa/New Zealand

To a lesser extent, the rhetoric of the 'war on crime' has reached across the Pacific. Still, in recent New South Wales elections, one party offered a 'three strikes and you're out' law-and-order platform and the other a 'one horrific crime and you're out' law-and-order platform. Just as in the US, to be seen to be 'tough on crime' is a vote winner. From 1980 to 1990 there has been a 59% increase in the number of uniformed police Australia-wide (Hampton 1994, p.7), increased prison terms and costly new prisons. The Australian prison population, at the 1982 census, was just under 10,000 and has now risen to over 15,800 (Mukherjee & Dagger 1993, p.23).

In Western Australia, US-style boot-camps, as described above, have been introduced for young offenders. What's more, with the increasing costs of imprisonment, rather than changing sentencing legislation, governments have opted to instead privatise prisons to a greater extent than anywhere else in the world. The privatisation of punishment has a long history - in England up until the 1790s the following practice was commonplace:

On entering the Bishop of Ely's lockup, a prisoner was chained down to the floor with a spiked collar riveted round his neck until he disgorged a fee for 'easement of irons'. Any jailer could load any prisoner with as many fetters as he pleased and charge for their removal one at a time. (Hughes 1987, p.37)

As Christie points out 'transportation was a result of private initiative and business instincts' (1993, p.119). Although current trends may be driven by very different circumstances, it seems that history has illustrated the ways in which privatisation creates an inevitable conflict of interest. Private prison operators profit from keeping people in prison rather than finding ways of returning them to their communities.

In Aotearoa/New Zealand, while the political rhetoric has been somewhat different in other countries above, the actual situation remains very similar. As long ago as 1980, successive ministers of justice have campaigned to reduce the number of people in prison. In 1989 Sir Clinton Roper chaired an inquiry entitled the 'Prison System Review' which recommended using prisons only as a last resort and instead creating a parallel system of sanction that dealt with the causes of offending - a nationwide series of 'habilitation' centres.

Seven years on, however, the first pilot schemes are yet to be underway and Aotearoa/New Zealand's rate of imprisonment remains well ahead of Australia's and that of most of the Western world. The number of New Zealanders in prison has risen 223% from 1981. In 1991 there were over 8,200 people incarcerated. In comparison to the USA, these figures are low but in all three countries the trends point to increasing numbers of people behind bars (Rosenblatt 1995).

7

Who is imprisoned?
Exploring issues of class and culture

The USA

Who are these thousands, indeed millions of people in prisons? Where are they from, and for what reason are they incarcerated? As mentioned earlier, Eddie Ellis served twenty-three years in the New York prison system and is now, with others in Harlem, New York, developing the 'Non-Traditional Approach to Criminal and Social Justice' (see chapter 15). In the interview below he declared that truth telling is the starting point in bringing about change to the US prison system - truth telling about who is imprisoned.[1]

Prison has become a place where all social problems can be put in a very profitable context. That colours the way people in prison are being treated. Corrections may overtake the defence system as the economic base of this country. The military industrial complex is being replaced by the prison industrial complex.

You are entered into a national computer system, can't afford bail or an attorney, so an incompetent or overworked attorney is allocated. Inevitably it results in some plea bargain, accommodation with the court. You plead guilty for a reduction of whatever sentence you were facing. You spend time. And because the prisons have become less and less places where you can make any sort of fundamental changes in your life and the rate of recidivism [returning to prison] is over 50%, it's like a very vicious cycle. Once labelled an ex-convict your chances for employment, for success in this country, your economic opportunities are greatly reduced and you become almost forced to engage in activities that are not legal. Inevitably this leads to offences, convictions and prison sentences.

Seventy-five percent of all those arrested are on drug offences - are victims of the 'war on drugs'. You might think that almost exclusively people of colour use drugs but according to the major drug agency in the USA - the Drug Enforcement Administration - the majority of people who buy drugs and use drugs are white. In New York State 75% of drug users are white middle-class people earning over $25,000 or better who live in the suburbs. Over half those who sell drugs fit the same profile. But when it comes to convictions and sentences white people total only 9% of those in prison.

Obviously the arrest for sale and possession of drugs is a selective kind of process and when white people are convicted they plead guilty to using and go to alternatives to incarceration such as the Betty Ford Clinic, while Blacks and Latinos go to prison. The system has been able to utilise this war on drugs as a methodology whereby large numbers of people in the inner city are picked up, convicted and sent to prison to feed the prison industrial complex. A lot of people profit from the building of a prison except those generally sent to prison. They are sent not because they are criminal but because they are undesirable. If you were really talking about sending drug criminals to prison then the complexion of prisons would be very different.   •

The economy, media, academics, politicians and police have created a criminal class. Having done so, America now dehumanises this class, demonises it. When you think of any of these people you think of a person who is not quite a human being, who you wouldn't want to be in an elevator with. Through the use of words like 'wolf-pack', 'savage', 'animalistic', they portray certain mental pictures that we have been bombarded with over the last twenty years, they are firmly in our minds.

Certain code words are used so that our politicians don't actually have to say who they are talking about. 'Tough on crime' translates into tough on Black people, Latino kids. 'Crime is running wild' means African American and Latino men are running wild. It is clearly understood. We have a crime bill of $32 billion that means get tough on Blacks and Latino kids.

In the introduction to Ward Churchill's book, *Cages of Steel*, which he titled 'The Third World at Home', Ward listed the injustices of the make-up of the US prison population:

> *As of 1980, by the government's own statistics, African Americans comprised eleven percent of the overall population, while the Black proportion of the aggregate US prison population was forty-four percent, and rising. By 1990, the proportion was over fifty percent and still rising. At the present rate of Black incarceration - which is six times the rate for whites - one in every four Afro American males will go to prison at least once during his life. Many will do time more than once ... If the present upward trend holds, as it has for sixty years ... half of all African American males will go to prison by the end of the present decade. For American Indian men, the rate is already one in every 3.5, and also rising. Latinos currently fill prison cells at a rate double their proportion of society as a whole, and their rate of incarceration too is increasing steadily. The number and proportion of women of color in prison is also rising sharply ... Official statistics reveal that non-whites consistently receive sentences thirty percent more severe than Euroamericans upon conviction for identical offences. People of color are at least twenty-five percent less likely than whites in similar circumstances to receive early parole. About fifty percent of all prisoners on death row are ... people of color, although whites are convicted of some two-thirds of all capital crimes.* (Churchill, in Churchill & Vander Wall 1992, p.12)

Australia

The situation in Australia is shockingly similar, as Ray Jackson, the Chairperson of the New South Wales Aboriginal Deaths In Custody Watch Committee, describes:[2]

> *We have our frustrations with the police. There are real problems with police bashings. We've got a bashings file that's pretty thick. I don't say that the bashings are increasing but the reporting of police bashings is increasing. The file just keeps getting bigger and bigger. They are an entire culture of their own making and have been for over 200 years. They were the original troopers in this country. They were the ones who took the children away from the families - the mothers and that. They*

were the ones who used to just ride out and shoot everybody. They were doing that early this century. Even up to the 1940s and '50s there are reports, especially up in the Northern Territory, of white patrol officers, whatever they call them up there, when they used to go around and do the thousand mile inspection of their area and they used to just go into a camp and pick up a 14 and 15 year-old girl and just drag her out, and if she got pregnant then that's just bad luck you know. They'd just drop her back home when they'd finished. That's just 40 or 50 years ago - within living memory. Nothing's ever said about it, nothing's ever done about it. They talk about war crimes. They talk about bloody war crimes. We've had it for 200 years.

Thirty five percent of young people in juvenile justice centres in New South Wales are Koori. The cops have a lot to do with that. They pick kids up at Bourke - they go on street sweeps, 'There's three - one, two, three', they put them before the magistrate, give some bullshit story and before you know it they're down here in Sydney. Their parents sometimes don't even know that they've gone until they ring from Yasmar or Minda[3] or wherever.

And then there's the racism both in the jails and in the courts. In the courts, magistrates are placing impossible bail conditions in a lot of cases and that's where they allow bail. We had the case of a 19 year-old and they banged on a $3,000 bail. Where's a 19 year-old going to get $3,000? You'd be flat out getting 3,000 cents! There's a definite bias against our people when they're up before the magistrates and judges. As soon as the police prosecutor denies bail, bang! - straight into custody. Pat O'Shane[4] and maybe one or two others are the only ones who argue against the police prosecutors and because the others don't, most of our people just automatically wind up out in jail.

Rather than accepting and implementing the recommendations of the Royal Commission[5] the arrest rates are still going up through the roof and that goes for our young people as well. Then when they get to court ... a magistrate made a statement in the paper a few weeks back that he categorically believed the police prosecutor and police witnesses at all times. He was shocked at the outcome of the Wood Commission[6] when police said that they lied and fabricated evidence. He was amazed and felt guilty to all those people he'd sent to prison. Well bad luck! Well I mean, Jesus, how much intelligence does it take to know what was going on and has been going on in this country for 200 years, for Christ sakes. If you don't fit into that mainstream culture, the establishment

*culture, then you just get sausaged through. That's you finished. For a
magistrate who is not that far up the ladder to be brainwashed that
much, if they believe everything that the police prosecutor tells them, it's
a wonder there aren't more people in jail! It's a joke!*

Indigenous Australians are 14 times more likely than non-Indigenous
Australians to find themselves in prison (Hampton 1994, p.11). One of the key
recommendations of the Royal Commission into Aboriginal Deaths in Custody
(November 1987 to 31 December 1990), was for Indigenous Australians to be
incarcerated only as a last resort. Since the Royal Commission however,
incarceration rates of Indigenous Australians have increased rather than
decreased, in some areas by up to eighty percent (Pilger 1992, p.355).

Many Indigenous Australians now in prison grew up in institutions due
to previous government policies of enforced separation of Indigenous
Australian children from their families. Indigenous Australians point to how
policing and imprisonment have become the present-day version of genocidal
practices (see *Dulwich Centre Newsletter*, 1995, No.1).

Imprisoning the unemployed

The 1993 Australian Prison Census found that of those prisoners
surveyed, only 4% had completed secondary school and at the time of arrest,
approximately 71% were unemployed (Mukherjee & Dagger 1993, p.23). The
link between unemployment and imprisonment is well known:

*If you go back in history and plot the population of all prisons ... and
compare it to all the other variables you can think of, you will find a
positive correlation only with unemployment. The higher the rate of
joblessness, the higher the rate of prison commitments. There is no
question about it.* (Norman Carlson, Director, US Prisons, cited in
Lichtenstein & Kroll 1995, p.14)

Aotearoa/New Zealand

In Aotearoa/New Zealand the picture is familiar, according to the
Justice Department's pen portrait of the 'average' prisoner:

*Aged 27, three-quarters are single, divorced, separated or widowed.
About two-thirds are beneficiaries* [welfare recipients], *three-quarters*

unemployed, half have severe alcohol and/or drug problems (two thirds of women inmates), half have had psychiatric assessment, half come from broken homes, nine out of ten have no formal qualifications, and only a handful own their own homes or have significant assets. A little fewer than half are Pakeha, the rest Polynesian. (Consedine 1995, p.30)

The crimes that lead to imprisonment

In considering which crimes lead to imprisonment, it seems relevant to first question the notion of 'crime':

I hesitate to use the word 'crime', because in a way 'crime' does not exist. It is just a social definition of certain unwanted acts. Sometimes there is no official action at all following such acts. Look at family matters - teenagers often act in ways that, if it were outside the family, would be labelled as 'crime', but because it is inside it's just your son who takes some money from the kitchen table or is hitting his brother. You don't call that 'theft' or 'violence' because you know reasons for his behaviour; but if it were a new neightbour's son you might assume he had a tendency for stealing. (Christie, in Swift 1996a, p.10)

Crime is in many ways a subjective term. When considering the differences between who commits the most harm in the culture, and who is imprisoned, this becomes more clear:

The greatest evil is not done in those 'sordid dens of crime' that Dickens loved to paint. It is not even done in concentration camps and labour camps. In these we see its final result. But it is conceived and ordered, moved, seconded, carried and minuted in clean, carpeted, warmed and well lighted offices, by quiet men with white collars, cut fingernails and smooth shaven cheeks, who do not need to raise their voices. (Lewis 1961, p.44)

These men do not make up prison populations. The crimes of the rich such as breaches of occupational health and safety regulations, price fixing, devastation of the environment, dispossession of Indigenous peoples' lands, the marketing and sale of outdated, ineffective, unnecessary or otherwise hazardous drugs by pharmaceutical companies, deceptive advertising, tax avoidance, stock market takeovers, fraudulent bankruptcies, the manufacture and trade of weapons of mass destruction, and even the invasion of countries, are rarely deemed illegal, let alone policed, nor do they result in incarceration. Abuses of power through industry, the media, armed forces, bureaucracies or legal systems rarely result in imprisonment. These are the crimes of the wealthy.

Even when the powerful commit the same crimes as the powerless they are far less likely to be imprisoned - physical or sexual assaults committed by the police, or by staff within other institutions such as the church, detention centres, or even by men within the family are less likely to result in incarceration than when they occur in other circumstances. When wealthy men commit crimes of violence (it is usually men) their access to resources and judicial bias often lead to non-custodial sentences.

The majority of people who are in prison are not there because of violent crimes. In Australia only 34.2% of male prisoners are imprisoned for homicide, assault, sex offences or offences against another person. The figure drops further to 20% for Australian women prisoners. Most men who are violent are not in prison. Most cases of sexual assault, child sexual assault, and domestic violence, are not prosecuted, and imprisonment is rare.

The crimes that most often result in imprisonment are crimes of property and drug offences. In Australia, 'break and enter' is the single most common cause of imprisonment. The most common offences that men in Australian prisons have committed are break and enter, robbery, dealing/trafficking drugs, and driving offences. For women prisoners, fraud and misappropriation, break and enter, robbery, dealing/trafficking drugs and 'other offences' (drunkenness or prostitution) make up the majority of their convictions (Mukherjee & Dagger 1993, p.43).

In the US, people are increasingly imprisoned for drug offences. Over a third of all felony convictions by 1988 were for drug offences (Mauer 1995, p.37). Many people use drugs, many men commit acts of violence, many people commit acts of theft, but overwhelmingly, around the western world, it is the relatively powerless who are imprisoned.

Before we consider how such a situation can continue with so little public outcry, it is important to first explore issues of gender and imprisonment. This is because it is overwhelmingly men who are imprisoned, and the following chapter attempts to make some sense of the complex social factors that lead to this being the case.

Notes

1 This interview took place in the Harlem Neighbourhood Defender's Office in August 1995.

2 This interview took place in the Aboriginal Deaths in Custody office in Sydney, Australia, in November 1995.

3 Yasmar and Minda are juvenile detention centres in Sydney, Australia.

4 Pat O'Shane was Australia's first Indigenous Australian magistrate.

5 Royal Commission into Aboriginal Deaths in Custody (November 1987 to 31 December 1990).

6 1996 Royal Commission into corruption within the New South Wales Police Force.

8

Who is imprisoned?
Exploring issues of masculinity

In Australia, at the 1993 census, men made up 95% of the prison population. Out of a total of 15,860 prisoners, 15,096 were men and 764 women (Mukherjee & Dagger 1993, p.23). In the US the percentages are similar (Kurshan 1995, p.114). This chapter tries to make sense of these figures.

Women before the courts

There is no evidence to suggest that women get off lightly before the courts. In fact, women are more likely to go to jail for a first offence than men. In addition, lack of child-care for those sentenced to community-based orders means that women are in danger of breaching the order and being sent to prison. There is evidence to suggest that judges and magistrates judge women before them on the basis of how well the woman fits into their stereotyped notions ... The overwhelming majority of women sent to prison have been convicted of property crimes or driving offences. Only one in twenty women has been sentenced to prison for a violent offence, and in some of those instances the woman's crime has been to kill her male partner after enduring years of domestic violence ... Other offences for which women are sent to prison are drug trafficking or breaches of court orders. Women in prison are more likely

*to have committed a victimless crime, such as prostitution or possession
of drugs than male prisoners.* (McCulloch 1995, p.7)

As Jude McCulloch, a long-term member of Women Against Prison,
describes above, women experience considerable discrimination before the
courts. In order to explore why the differences in figures of incarceration for
men and women are so stark, the rest of this chapter focuses on the ways in
which constructions of masculinity relate to culture and class and, in turn, how
these relate to crime and imprisonment. It aims to explore how it can be that
men commit the vast majority of crimes in our culture, and how it can be that
prisons are overwhelmingly filled with men from working-class backgrounds
and men of colour.

Masculinities, crime and imprisonment

Growing up as a man I found myself within an all-boys private school,
saturated in particular messages of masculinity: of competition, winning and
dominating others. Fate and my white, middle-class privilege allowed me to
largely succeed at those markers of identity that were required for 'manhood':
football, academic success and an ability to lie about one's sexual practices. At
the same time the loneliness and cruelty of men's culture left me baffled and
disillusioned. By the time I was in my final year of schooling it was the
friendship of boys in younger years that was keeping me afloat. They still
seemed to have a spark of life within their eyes.

It was largely through relationships with women whom I loved - my
mother, sisters, friends and partners - that space was opened for me to step into
ways of being that were forbidden in a masculine world. And it was through the
challenges of my older sister and the writings of feminist women that I could
start to make sense of the culture of men. At the same time my father's
challenges to the status quo through his involvement in anti-nuclear protest, and
his questioning, caring mind, always invited me to think that there must be
other ways forward.

Beginning to see the real effects of men's ways of being, but also
finding excitement in talking and working with men differently, led me into
work with young men in schools on issues of gender and violence (see
Denborough 1995). My work in prisons offered me an opportunity to try to
give back some of the hope that these young men once offered me. In many
ways, choosing to work within a men's maxi-mum security prison was due to

wanting to know more about the most masculine insti-tution in our culture. My first crucial learning was the fact that men like me, white middle-class men, are not within the prison system.

Constructions of masculinity

As described in previous chapters, there are particular crimes that result in imprisonment and particular communities and groups of men that are policed and imprisoned for these crimes. Not only is it overwhelmingly poor and dispossessed men who are imprisoned, it is also *young* men from these communities - at least at the time of their first sentence. Between 15-24 are the peak years for the committal of the sorts of crimes that result in imprisonment (Mauer 1995, p.33).

The dominant constructions of masculinity in our culture that I experienced myself, and have since witnessed in schools throughout cities and country towns, privilege the importance of dominating and controlling others, climbing hierarchies and obtaining possessions. At the same time, as feminist writers have documented over the last twenty years, these dominant ways of being a man also justify the use of coercion, force, and in many cases even violence to achieve such control and power.

Young men receive these messages in a context of relative powerlessness. Most young people in our culture are without financial independence, have little control over their own learning, and often spend much of their waking hours within rigid hierarchical institutions (schools). Young men receive the dominant gender messages that they ought to dominate and control others in this context. In this atmosphere, the messages are understandably powerful and seductive. If young men are able to position themselves within the dominant ways of being a man, they gain attention, air space, and a greater say (power) over their lives and those of others. At the very least they are less likely to be targets of abuse, and will themselves have easy targets to pick on.

The options available for young men to create particular ways of being men are enormously influenced by issues of class and race. As a white middle-class young man, within a private school, I had a clear line to status and prestige through future study and opportunities for wealth. Within an individualistic and highly competitive climate, both academically and in sports, I could compete and stand a very good chance of winning. For white middle-class boys such as myself, where achievements within school are not enough to shore up a masculine identity, minor acts outside of school with peers often suffice - such as drinking, pranks, or vandalism (Messerschmidt 1993, p.94-5): Within the white middle-class masculine youth culture from which I came, attitudes to power and sexual conquest led to sexual coercion and date-rape of young women. At the same time, interpersonal physical violence was largely contained to the sporting field.

In many ways we were being trained to commit forms of crimes other than those that usually result in imprisonment - crimes of the stock-markets, in the boardrooms and in the bedrooms with future partners. We were being trained and given access to other opportunities for control and domination - through the power of industry, finances, media, bureaucracies, the armed forces and the law. In the public arena we were offered open doors to realms of power and therefore had little need to prove ourselves on the streets. Similarly with access to resources, our drug-taking or risk-taking had little chance of being noticed by the police. Even if it had been, with our connections, the possibilities of imprisonment would have remained distant.

For other young men these doors to power are hidden or firmly locked. Young men from working-class communities and communities of colour receive similar over-riding cultural messages in relation to the need to individually achieve, to climb the hierarchies and obtain the possessions, but have little or no possibility of fulfilling these forms of masculinity. Other forms of identity, of power, of excitement and of pleasure must be found. With no access to property, the street often becomes the focus for activity. For many, street crime and drugs become two of very few options available in order to achieve status, control and a sense of masculinity and acceptance. And street crime, unlike other crime, is stringently policed.

At the same time, finding themselves locked out of the mainstream can bring outrage, especially for young men of colour who find themselves constantly confronting racist institutions and individuals. Quite apart from these factors and their contribution to some forms of crime, many young men from poor communities become involved in crimes of property purely and simply for the money when there is little hope of obtaining considerable resources in any other way.

A substantial amount of street crime that results in imprisonment is in many ways resistance to social inequities. These inequities affect young working-class men and young men of colour who resist in often highly visible ways. Their actions are subsequently policed and result in incarceration. Without access to other so-called 'legitimate' (middle-class) ways of being men, finding themselves outside of the mainstream, some young men from working-class communities and communities of people of colour, create powerful identities of resistance, in which street crime plays an important part. In this way, the sense of excitement and adventure deemed so crucial to masculine ideals can be achieved without the access to resources that might otherwise be necessary.

Throughout the culture, in all communities, dominant constructions of masculinity also lead to crimes of violence between men and by men against women and children. It is generally working-class men who are imprisoned for these crimes. As is the case with all crimes, wealthy men often find alternative avenues open to them due to their access to resources, support, references and judicial prejudice.

It is overwhelming men who are imprisoned. Men from working-class communities and men of colour end up in front of the courts for pursuing the very forms of masculinity that our culture applauds in a whole variety of ways, whether through the glorification of physical violence in movies and 'contact' sports, or the celebration of the 'killer instinct' in politicians, business executives and sports stars. They may believe that physical violence is the only avenue open to them to attain the power and status open to middle-class men in a variety of other, more acceptable - though not necessarily less destructive - ways.

9

Silencing the politics
of imprisonment

How can it be that our culture allows the incarceration of the poor, the young, the Indigenous, at such alarming rates without so much as a murmur? In order to explore the cultural silences that surround the politics of imprisonment, this chapter turns to a particular interpretation of the history of the prison. This interpretation is only one of many, and I review it here because it has been particularly helpful for me in exploring how issues of crime have been individualised, the politics hidden, and why local communities no longer address their own conflicts.

Histories and heresies of imprisonment

After the War of Independence in the United States of America, Britain, in 1788, turned to Australia as a site for the transportation of prisoners. The poorest were sent here, and, in the process, the Indigenous peoples of this continent were imprisoned too, within white ways, and at the barrel of my ancestors' guns. A tradition of resolving conflicts was imposed on this land from England, and Indigenous customary law was forbidden.

Within Britain, prior to the Norman Invasion, a crime was something to be resolved between the offender, the victim, their families and the local community. This state of affairs was challenged, however, by William the Conqueror and his descendants when they found the legal process an effective tool for centralising their own political authority. They competed with the church's influence over secular matters and effectively replaced local systems of dispute resolution (van Ness, Carlson, Crawford & Strong 1994, p.13).

In 1116, William the Conqueror's son, Henry I, issued the *Leges Henrici*, which secured royal jurisdiction over certain offences against the king's peace - arson, robbery, murder, false coinage, and crimes of violence. The king became the primary victim in criminal offences and the actual victim lost their position and any meaningful voice in the justice process (van Ness, Carlson, Crawford & Strong 1994, p.13).

I have found Michel Foucault's explorations of the meanings of this historical change particularly helpful:

> *The right to punish ... [became] an aspect of the sovereign's right to make war on his enemies ... by breaking the law, the offender has touched the very person of the prince; and it is the prince - or at least those to whom he has delegated his force - who seizes upon the body of the condemned man and displays it marked, beaten, broken. The ceremony of punishment, then is an exercise in 'terror' ... to make everyone aware, through the body of the criminal, of the unrestrained presence of the sovereign.* (Foucault 1977, pp.48-9)

According to Foucault, in this way the 'body of the condemned' became the site for state torture, punishment and public executions. Punishment was visible and obvious, a 'spectacle' to behold. The public had ceased being a part of the decision-making process of restoring justice but remained as witnesses, as an intricate part of the execution of punishment. This began to change in Europe in the late 18th century as resistance grew:

> *The people never felt closer to those who paid the penalty than in those rituals intended to show the horror of the crime and the invincibility of power; never did the people feel more threatened, like them, by a legal violence exercised without moderation or restraint. The solidarity of a whole section of the population with those we would call petty offenders - vagrants, false beggars, the indigent poor, pick-pockets, receivers and dealers in stolen goods - was constantly expressed: resistance to police searches, the pursuit of informers, attacks on the watch or inspectors provide abundant evidence of this. And it was the breaking up of this solidarity that was becoming the aim of penal and police repression.* (Foucault 1977, p.63)

Foucault describes that the horror of the gallows was creating circumstances in which at times the crowd turned against the state, and the executioner became the criminal. As I understand it, he argues that this was one reason why 'reforms' of the 18th and 19th centuries moved technologies of punishment out of the public arena, away from blatant torture of the body and instead towards the less visible - imprisonment. The condemned was no longer to be seen, and punishment was to become the most hidden part of the penal process.

Whether or not these examples of protest against public punishment were commonplace, and there certainly seems to exist evidence of contradictions, I have found this story illuminating. When walking into prisons it seems to me as if they are institutions perfectly designed to hide the real effects of their practices from the broader community.

The birth of the prison

In this context the prison was born and punishment began to target not only the body but also the 'soul' or spirit of the prisoner, as Blanche Hampton describes:

Imprisonment controls and affects the spirit. That's why they do it - because it does work. That's why they lock you up, because it does affect the spirit - that's the point, that's the punishment. If you look at the original idea of the penitentiary, that's what it was for, for you to become penitent. (in conversation, 1996)

Imprisoning the poor

According to Karlene Faith (1993, p.121), the concept of the prison built upon the English traditions of the poorhouses, workhouses and houses of correction. These had been established in pre-industrialised England as a way of *removing undesirable elements from the streets or new urban centres and ostensibly reforming idle or deviant citizens by teaching them the discipline and habits of hard work* (Faith 1993, p.121). Faith describes these poorhouses as the 'precursors of prisons' and argues that they served to warehouse people who were stigmatised as unruly, or dangerous classes.

The birth of 'the criminal'

Foucault (1977, p.93) proposed that addressing crimes, in some ways, became less important than the 'criminality' of the offenders. New knowledges and processes were constructed, detailed laws and regulations were laid down, and judges began to assess not only the guilt or innocence of those before them, but their propensity to repent, re-offend, and/or be rehabilitated. Judges, and others involved in the justice system, began to assess degrees of a person's 'criminality'. The person before them ceased to be someone who had committed a crime and instead became a 'criminal'. It became understood that:

[there exists a] *disturbed and incurable criminal class, marked by low physical and mental characteristics; that crime is hereditary in the families of criminals belonging to this class; and that hereditary crime is a disorder of mind, having close relations of nature and descent to epilepsy, dipsomania, insanity and other forms of degeneracy. Such criminals are really morbid varieties, and often exhibit marks of physical degeneration - spinal deformities, stammering, imperfect organs of speech, club foot, cleft palate, harelip, deafness, paralysis, epilepsy and scrofula.* (Hampton 1994, p.59)

So uttered Mr Thompson, Surgeon to the General Prison of Scotland towards the end of the nineteenth century. The birth of the medical and psychological professions which offered, and continue to offer, new 'norms' by which to judge individuals was crucial in this process of individualising crime. The norms of white, middle-class, and invariably male professionals focused on, and created, the 'criminal' behind the crime.

If radio programs are anything to go by, contemporary versions of Mr Thompson's medical causes of criminality are deeply entrenched. In the last month I have accidentally tuned into two relevant programs, one of which had two doctors proudly proclaiming how their latest book demonstrates the physiological differences between criminals and law-abiding citizens, and why they should be asked to assess difficult children at school. The other program confidently stated that the 'latest research' has found that 'criminals' have more children than 'normal' people. Individualistic views of crime now have considerable influence as demonstrated by diagnostic criteria such as the DSM-III-R and its creation of 'oppositional defiant disorders' and 'conduct disorders' which have taken 'criminal activity' into the field of mental health knowledges.[1]

The birth of correction

These individualistic understandings of crime and 'criminals' disguise the fact that people are often punished for resisting social inequities, and imply instead that they are being offered the 'correction' or therapy which they require in order to fit within mainstream culture. These languages of correction also relieve judges of declaring their role as punishers: *do not imagine that the sentences that we judges pass are activated by a desire to punish; they are intended to correct, reclaim, 'cure'* (Foucault 1977, p.10). The entire function of the criminal justice system - to punish - becomes disguised.

This increases the effects of state power. According to Foucault, it enables the state *not to punish less, but to punish better; to punish with an attenuated severity perhaps, but in order to punish with more universality and necessity; to insert the power to punish more deeply into the social body* (1977, p.82).

In this context prisons need not correct, they need only create the illusion that all people within their walls need individual 'correction'. And this prison systems do all too well:

> *Just the very fact that they call us 'inmate' ... it says that you are flawed, there's something wrong with you. You're an inmate and this is a hospital; this is going to make you well. Well, this isn't a hospital and I'm not flawed. I'm not an inmate. I'm not sick. And there's nothing here being done to make me any better.* (an anonymous prisoner, cited in Prison Research Education Action Project 1976, p.10)

In these ways the obvious injustices of the criminal justice and penal systems as described in previous chapters are disguised and most citizens simply see prisons as a response to crime and criminals. Issues of class, race and gender have become so obscured behind narrow definitions of criminality that we are able as a culture to over-whelmingly imprison working-class and Indigenous peoples. The realities of the prison system have become disguised to such an extent that we confuse locking people in cells for years at a time, exposing them to violence, punishment, degradation and abuse, with, of all things, correction.

The political ramifications are many and varied. The professions in which I have been trained - psychology and education, are deeply implicated in disguising the politics of imprisonment and the ways in which notions of punishment saturate our culture. Questioning this training, and the understandings and practices involved, opens the possibilities for action.

Note

1   Thousands of people within prison, and outside of prison, could now be diagnosed
under the following criteria for Conduct Disorder (cited in Christie 1993, p.157):

*A disturbance of conduct lasting at least six months, during which at least three
of the following have been present:*
   *(1)   has stolen without confrontation of a victim on more than one
          occasion (including forgery);*
   *(2)   has run away from home overnight at least twice while living in
          parental or parental surrogate home (or once without returning);*
   (3)   often lies (other than to avoid physical or sexual abuse);
   (4)   has deliberately engaged in fire-setting;
   (5)   is often truant from school (for older person, absent from work);
   (6)   has broken into someone else's house, building, or car;
   (7)   has deliberately destroyed others' property (other than by fire-setting);
   (8)   has been physically cruel to animals;
   (9)   has forced someone into sexual activity with him or her;
   (10) has used a weapon in more than one fight;
   (11) often initiates physical fights;
   *(12) has stolen with confrontation of a victim (e.g., mugging, purse-
          snatching, extortion, armed robbery);*
   (13) has been physically cruel to people.
*The conduct problems are more serious than those seen in Oppositional Defiant
Disorder.*

10

Imprisoning psychology
and education

One of the most difficult and confusing things for me to come to terms with while I was working in prisons was the gradual dawning of the ways in which professionals, including myself, become a part of imprisoning practices. One of the most disillusioning moments of my research occurred within a 'super maximum security control unit'[1]. Having been shown around this bunker, with its disinfectant-smelling floors and grey walls, having watched people in manacles constantly in isolation, and having witnessed the latest technologies of control and surveillance, I was in a state of shock. My body was clenched. There was a profound feeling of claustrophobia, of weight upon my being.

We had passed the self-contained hospital area, the beds with restraints attached, and were turning a corner when we passed a team of health professionals. Our tour guide asked if I would like to speak with them. At first I declined because I felt I would be incapable of communicating with anyone at that time, but on reflection I turned back in the hope of making a connection within the walls.

After brief introductions I asked them, 'What are some of the mental health issues that you have to deal with in a climate like this?' I was expecting them to speak of the sensory deprivation, the self-hatred, the hopelessness; or perhaps the ways people resist the system or take this out on themselves through acts of self-harm. Instead I listened as they described the psychiatric conditions that most of those incarcerated bring with them to prison: 'conduct disorders, personality disorders, oppositional disorders, anger-management problems'.

One of the workers had come up with an award-winning anger management program that they conducted through video into each of the cell televisions. The prisoners never meet one another and this way is cost-effective. If they don't watch the TV and do the exercises this will provide good reason to hold them for longer. There is a high rate of viewing and completion of the exercises. The statistics look good.

I heard how mental health workers are involved in devising individual 'behaviour management programs' for prisoners who are disruptive. As far as I could see, these add up to a psychological torture routine, depriving prisoners of those things that are calculated to be most important to them.

I asked, in a quiet voice, whether many people incarcerated here attempt suicide or harm themselves. They replied with a great deal of satisfaction that, no, this didn't occur, that they had solved this problem by not responding to 'manipulative behaviour', and anyway 'there is nothing to use to harm yourself here'.

I was speechless. I did not respond. I was paralysed and overwhelmed. I colluded in silence. I stayed quiet and continued walking through the institution. Being within such a place, witnessing its destructiveness, and the part played by my own profession, upset me so much that I could find no way to challenge it. I was just one more visitor taken on a tour of the institution. If I had spoken out there would have been no risk to me.

If I had tried to express how filled with rage I would become if I was incarcerated in that place, and heard professionals talking in these ways, nothing terrible would have happened to me if I, as a visitor, had spoken out about this. If I had tried to convey my understanding that no anger management program would make the slightest difference to my state of mind if I was never allowed to talk to another person, if I never felt the sun on my skin, if I spent 23 hours a day in a concrete box, I would still have been allowed out the front door. Within the control unit I couldn't find the words to speak, but prisoners do, and when they articulate the outrage they are further pathologised and controlled. Indeed that is often why they have been placed in the control unit in the first place.

When I left the institution I was shaking. I am not sure whether this was because of the effects of being in such a place, or whether it was a consequence of my silence and my body trying to come to terms with its meaning. That night I could not sleep and began instead to write. I wrote the previous page. It was the first writing I did for this publication. It was also a turning-point. It marked the end of my silence. I could not think of the faces of the men and women incarcerated in that place and remain silent. What's more, it brought home to me all the times in the past that I had not spoken of the outrage of prison. It reminded me of all the times I had colluded through silence, and the times I did protest but did not push the point for fear of losing my job - the times I sat in front of the superintendent unable to find words. I recalled the time when another worker did find her voice and lost her job and I did not stand with her. I recalled the times I tried to work within and through the mazes of injustice and in the end felt washed up, lost, of no use to those within prison, and yet continuing to take the pay packet. I recalled the times I carried home my outrage and left it in my body rather than finding ways to take action. I recalled sitting quietly in staff meetings. I recalled standing silently in the control unit hearing the justifications for what is clearly torture - sensory deprivation within a concrete bunker, shackles and prolonged solitary confinement. Playing my part in this publication is my first response to such memories.

Within Australia

In the control unit it was obvious how psychological understandings were being used to disguise political processes and dynamics of power. This also seems to be true throughout the Australian and Aotearoa/New Zealand prison systems - even in circumstances where we as practitioners are genuinely dedicated to improving the lives of those with whom we are working. Over the last ten years psychological programs within prisons have become held up as the hopeful intervention or 'rehabilitation' for prisoners.

Many prisoners and ex-prisoners have other ideas. Blanche Hampton, in her book *No Escape: Prisons, Therapy and Politics,* describes the power that therapists hold over prisoners' lives:

> *If therapists in the community have the authority of their expertise, therapists in prison have the added power of the weight of their reports to inmate classification committees.* (1994, p.9)

In the following interview Blanche speaks with considerable outrage about the role of psychology within prisons.[2]

Some years after I left prison I heard that the self-mutilation rate had gone up enormously. Now I was out I became totally caught up in it. I guess part of me saw it as a way to assuage my guilt that I felt for all the times when I hadn't done it, all the times when I had said nothing. I thought, now here is an opportunity to say something, and I must say something because they haven't got control of me at the moment and I can do that. And I got so totally caught up in it, I began to identify so deeply with what was happening, that I became very, very borderline. I was in deep depression for about a year. It left me feeling very hollow and not even angry, too distraught to even be angry.

I had to do No Escape *at the time because I was contracted. I thought it was terribly important to do it. At the time I had been alerted of the fact that slash-ups had increased by officers who couldn't bear working with it. I knew a lot of the professional staff there at the time, psychologists, education staff, but none of them spoke to me. When I checked with them about verifying what I had heard they all agreed. I spoke to them all separately and they all said this is terrible - 'you should do something about it'. Like I should do something about it! Great! I should do something about it. So I did. It got to the point where we had a background briefing radio program on the issue. They did a really good job and I asked a number of the workers to speak. They would have been unidentifiable. They would have changed their voices. They did that for a couple of people - officers again who had a conscience. But the professional staff wouldn't do it. All of them felt too ... I don't know, they were quite prepared to patch up the problem but they were not prepared to speak to stop it from happening. I found that totally disgusting.*

I mean, whose side are we on here? That was one of the reasons for the great sense of disillusionment and bitterness that I felt about it. I wanted to knock the 'professionals' off their moral high horse and say, hey, you've got all these women slashing up and you're not prepared to say anything - how bad does it have to get? To be left by the people who are supposed to be caring for them and their mental welfare, I found that appalling and I wanted to expose it for the fraud that it was.

I mean some professional staff personally believe that they are out there to save the women. That they are going to save the women. While they're out there saving them they were slashing up in the middle of the night.

I don't know how big a role education and psychology have in creating such a situation. But they started up a dream therapy session that they had no business running. I mean, who the hell has any qualification to run it anyway? They started up sexual abuse counselling that the women didn't want to go to and that the women were bullied into going to. You can't dig deep into somebody's psyche and then send them back to the wing after an hour. I mean, what are you going to do with them? You start unravelling bits of what has happened to them. You start making them feel that the only people that they've got outside for them, their family, have done bad things to them, then send them back to their cells to think about it, brood about it for the next twelve hours. They interpret aspects of your life as weaknesses even if they are the things that have enabled you to survive this long, that you might have died otherwise. You get no credit for even having stayed alive. You get no credit for the kids you may have raised, for whatever work you might have done, for the loyal friend that you are, for resistance to a system that has been grinding you down. You get no credit for any of that. All you are left with is a big bunch of negatives. And you're left to brood on that for a year or so while they whittle away your other defences. It really makes me angry.

There's almost a vampire-like quality of feeding off negatives. It's voyeuristic. I think workers within prison can become addicted in some way to the negative aspects. You can develop some sort of relish about hearing about pain and misery. You feed off that and you do damage to the people who you are taking that out on because you leave them with those thoughts to serve their sentence with. And in that context, when they are powerless to do anything about them anyway, that's a very nasty thing to do to another human being in the guise of helping them.

Therapeutic communities

Recently the notion and construction of 'therapeutic communities' has been hailed by many prison reformers as the radical progressive direction for the future. In these 'communities' prisoners are allowed to cook and clean for themselves and sometimes even wear their own clothes. They live together and often attempt to fulfil a number of psychological goals through the use of groups and individual counselling and educational programs. It is difficult to write critically of these programs, for often they represent respite from normal prison. They are places in which people are treated humanely, and where the lives and experiences of people in prison are listened to and taken seriously. I have spoken to numerous people who claim their lives have been radically improved by such programs.

They raise, however, serious political questions. The professionals, like me, who work in these settings are generally from cultures far removed from those of the prisoner population. Their assumptions and judgements are all based on ways of understanding the world that are very different from the prisoners' ways. Although 'therapeutic communities' are often more humane than regular prisons, and involve actually listening to the lives of prisoners, often the ways these lives are then understood are foreign to the communities which prisoners come from and to where they will return. Further distance is placed between prisoners and their families, histories and communities. What's more, all social factors of crime/life are silenced, leaving Indigenous peoples, people of colour, as well as those from communities affected by poverty, to have their lives and actions dissected in terms of 'self-esteem', 'conflict-resolution', or lack of parenting skills.

The situation for men incarcerated for violent crimes is similar. The rare work on issues of violence that does occur within prisons is overwhelmingly facilitated by white, middle-class professionals in ways that individualise the issues, obscure power relations of class, race and gender, and ignore the impact of the culture of prisons on men's violence. Men are often encouraged to view their violence in terms of an anger-management issue, a lack of communication skills, an issue of self-esteem, or individual pathology.

Prison is a place in which those incarcerated have to shut down and protect themselves, both from others and from overwhelming feelings of worthlessness, in order to survive. It is hardly an environment which encourages men who are violent to challenge their identity and practices of domination. It is hardly an environment that facilitates prisoners being able to open themselves to the feelings of others. As professionals we leave the prison each night, and those with whom we are working return to cells and a system designed to punish and prey upon feelings of guilt and worthlessness.

Teaching prisoners a lesson: Education in prison

Like psychology, the dominant educational discourses have a tendency to individualise the explanations for why people commit crimes and end up in prison. They regularly infer that people offend and re-offend because of educational deficits within themselves - deficits in cognition, life-skills, reading and writing, and in learning. Prisoners are often assessed as 'deficient', but access to the kinds of trades they wish to pursue is restricted and instead they are encouraged to work within prison factories, perhaps being trained at the same time. Often these industries are within prisons because the economy outside no longer sustains them. It is not uncommon for prisoners to be trained in work that only occurs within prisons! In sixteen state prison systems and the Federal system in the USA, basic education is now compulsory, while Pell Grants for tertiary study are no longer available to prisoners (Davidson 1995). People are forced to study what they may not want to study and are unable to study at higher levels.

At the same time, counsellors and teachers are increasingly employed directly by the Departments in charge of prisons, making it more difficult for individual workers to speak out publicly about prisons without threatening their jobs and livelihoods. Despite this, many of those working within prisons are aware of the injustices surrounding them, and are struggling to overcome the constraining contexts to find ways of making a difference.

In many ways the dominant practices of psychology and education individualise crimes, de-politicise policing and imprisonment, and give the impression that prisons are places not of degradation but instead places of 'correction'. As a member of both the education and psychology professions - professions supposed to be 'correcting' - such realisations have challenged me to find new ways to understand both prisons and my work within them.

Notes:

1   I have chosen not to name the particular institution as the practices I witnessed within it are similar or the same as those within all prisons. To name individuals or even individual institutions would serve only to set myself apart from the practices in which we as professionals are all deeply implicated.

2   These passages are extracts from an interview which took place in Coogee, New South Wales, in November 1995.

11

The politics of punishment

Clint Deveaux is an African American judge in Atlanta Georgia. Below he describes how the US legal system is based on notions of retribution.[1]

Retribution is a basic tenet of the criminal system in America, there's no question about it. We see the court as acting instead of vigilantes, instead of a person who is harmed or injured or otherwise victimised - whether it's property or personal violence or some other offence against them. Instead of that person acting, the community acts in response to it. And the response is retributive. It is not designed to either understand or to restore. That may be a secondary goal but the first one is retribution. It is a problem for America because it is younger on these things than some other cultures. America broke away from the communitarian approach because it was so much bigger. I think this is the real reason for it. Because we don't take a communitarian approach we see the responsibility narrowly as only individual, and while I would agree that it's important for a person to be responsible for their own behaviour and to be in control of their own behaviour, not to be able to blame somebody else for it, it is equally critical that we have a clear understanding about the fact that none of us are in this world alone, and that everything about us is relationships, whether they are one-on-one or in groups, families, or larger groups like neighbourhoods or schools.

If a culture chooses a communitarian response, it will look to the effects of a criminal justice system on the entire community, not just make retributive decisions on individuals. If the idea is to fix the victim so that the damage is restored, and then to do something to repair what damage may have been done to the sense of community, then our approach would be very different. (in conversation, 1996)

A punitive culture

The Australian system seems little different. We live within a punitive culture - one that often equates justice with revenge, in which many relationships end in retribution, and in which ways of addressing conflict often inflame anguish rather than diminish it. From child-rearing practices, to the schoolyard, to the courts, we are steeped in notions of punishment - that somehow, in order to 'resolve conflict', the punishment of those who have caused harm or displayed disobedience is all-important. Even the 'value-free science' of behaviourism, while not directly involving itself with notions of punishment, seems to verge perilously close to them in its development of deprivation behaviour management practices.

The roots of such punitive ways of thinking and living, I imagine, would vary enormously throughout different cultures. In this chapter I have chosen to explore Judeo-Christian traditions, because they form an important cultural thread within dominant Western societies and cultures. My primary source for this discussion has been the writing of a European man, Philip Greven. I have found his thoughts and writings revealing in coming to understand more fully the often punitive nature of Judeo-Christian-based culture. While punishment seems to be embedded in many religious traditions, including Christianity, it is important to stress that within these traditions there have always been people and groups who have actively opposed such directions, and sought to develop alternatives:

Punishment is embedded in most Christian theology. The threat of future and eternal punishment has provided the ineradicable core of violence, suffering and pain that has perpetuated anxiety and fear in the minds of vast numbers of people throughout the world for two millennia ... For many Christians ... hell is an actual, physical place of punishment, the locale of future suffering so vast, so extreme, and so permanent that our minds can hardly grasp the enormity of the threat. (Greven 1992, p.55)

This belief system translates into the everyday world in many ways including child-rearing practices:

The terror of eternal punishment has always been at the root of much suffering on this earth as well. Incalculable suffering and pain have been inflicted on children because of the belief in the physical reality of hell. Many Christians have heeded and acted upon the words of Proverbs 23:13-14: 'Withhold not correction from the child: for if thou beatest him with the rod, he shall not die. Thou shalt beat him with the rod, and shalt deliver his soul from hell.' (Greven 1992, p.60)

These doctrines have had extensive secular influence, and notions of punishment have at times been almost synonymous with discipline and childrearing in our culture. Many parents still believe that physical punishment is a useful 'last resort', although such attitudes have been widely challenged in recent times by more and more parents and educators. According to Greven, the beliefs underlying the traditional approach to corporal punishment of children were as follows:

The spanking should be administered firmly. It should be painful and it should last until the child's will is broken. It should last until the child is crying, not tears of anger but tears of a broken will. As long as he is stiff, grits his teeth, holds on to his own will, the spanking should continue. (Jack Hyles, cited in Greven 1992, pp.68-69)

What are the effects of these notions of punishment, not only on the ways that individual children and adults see themselves? What are the effects of these notions of punishment on our culture and communities? How do they affect relationships between adults and young people? And how do they influence our responses to conflict? Do they restrain us from creating alternative responses to conflict that could build relationships rather than tearing them apart?

There are many parallels between the punishment of children and the ways in which our culture views the punishment of 'criminals'. Reverend Horace Bushnell, writing in the mid 1800s, described how the physical punishment of children 'turns the house into a penitentiary, or house of correction' (cited in Greven 1992, pp.89-90). Perhaps it is the wholesale acceptance of the punishment of children that enables our culture to imprison. With notions of punishment saturating our culture there is generally an unquestioned belief that if a crime or action that is harmful takes place, the individual or group involved must be punished. These notions inform taken-for-granted ways of being in our culture. Moreover, it is often believed that the more damage caused, the worse ought to be the punishment. So ingrained are these beliefs that at times they seem almost written in stone - 'God-given' perhaps.

Prison in many ways is representative of 'hell on earth'. It holds this place within our consciousness. It is held up as the result of disobedience to the laws of the state. Furthermore, like spanking, prisons were designed to break the will of the people. It is a common belief that prisons are terrible places but that they are necessary, like spanking.

The feminist movement, in its naming of issues of child abuse, and in the development of feminist parenting, have created space to challenge notions of punishment in our culture. Perhaps we will decide that, far from punishment protecting us as a culture, instead we need to be protected from notions of punishment. How to untangle ourselves from practices of punishment will be far from simple, however, as they so saturate our beings.

Away from punishing the young

Sharon Gollan, in the same interview from which extracts were included in chapter 3, describes moving away from notions of punishment as 'stepping out into the unknown':[2]

I just remember being called in to the school once with my nephew, who is five years old, and they were going to expel him for a week. I said: 'What will he learn from that? All he will learn - what you're already starting to teach him is that he is a 'bad' boy and that this is what happens when you are a 'bad' boy. I know he is not a bad boy.' So I said: 'I've been doing some things at home with him. Please don't expel him. Let me stay with him for a while. I actually want to talk with him about it.' And I talked to his teacher about what we were doing at home. He came home one day and said he had been a bad boy and that he was in trouble. I remember saying to him, 'How does that make you feel?' And he said, 'Unhappy', so we actually named it. We named it 'Trouble': 'So it was Trouble that made you unhappy today?' And so he started to make the disconnection between himself and being a bad boy. We began to create different stories for himself.

He was going off to school that very next day and I said: 'Well,
let's see what we can do with Trouble. Where shall we put him today?'
He drew Trouble and said, 'We'll put him on the fridge'. That's where
he wanted to leave him for that day. It's those sorts of stories we need
for young people at school, to be able to straight away begin to actually
deal with the problem themselves instead of generalising it and it
becoming them.

This story, and stories like this one, seem to step outside of traditional
notions of punishment and into different ways of speaking and thinking. These
alternative ways of thinking refuse to locate problems within individuals. They
instead 'externalise' problems so that people can work together against them.
These ways of working and thinking are discussed in more detail in chapter 14.[3]

Away from punishing ourselves

Within a punitive culture I imagine we are also invited to punish
ourselves. To what extent are levels of castigation and humiliation of others
influenced by our beliefs about ourselves and what we deserve?

I have wondered a great deal about the voice of self-punishment lately
as I have tried to find ways of restoring/transforming a friendship harmed as a
consequence of my actions. I have held various conversations with the voice of
self-punishment. He (the voice of punishment sounds masculine to me) has
encouraged me to search in isolation for all the ways I have hurt my friend, to
break my actions down, to feel what my friend must have felt at each step along
the way. He has encouraged stories of me that both deny aspects of myself and
discredit histories of the friendship. He believes that I deserve to feel as bad as,
or worse than, my friend did, that this is justice. All the while he refuses to see
any broader context for my actions. He encourages me to go over and over the
events, to dwell on my mistakes rather than focus on ways of moving forwards,
on ensuring harm does not happen again, of restoring the relationship. The
voice of punishment divides me from my friend.

Asking questions of the voice of self-punishment has been useful but
at times confusing. It is difficult for me sometimes to separate the voice of
punishment from one of 'responsibility'. Questions that are forward-looking
have proved unburdening - what steps would contribute to restoration, to truly
understanding what occurred and ensuring that it couldn't happen again? In
what ways could paths be created that honour my friend's experience in ways

that are unburdening? How can we build upon the aspects of our connection that always bring riches?

    If we began to speak about the voice of punishment in our own lives, I wonder if it would open space to challenge the punitive nature of our culture. I wonder if we would discover hidden histories of tussling with the voice of punishment and histories of finding ways to resist it. What would it mean if we started to share these stories? What are the alternative voices to the voice of punishment, and how could we collectively build upon them? These questions are considered in Part Three of this book, which explores non-punitive approaches to addressing crime and violence in our communities.

Notes:

1   This interview took place in Atlanta, Georgia, USA, in April 1996.

2   This interview took place at Dulwich Centre, Adelaide, South Australia, in early 1996.

3   For a detailed exploration of the ideas of externalising problems and alternative non-punitive approaches to addressing problems see White & Epston (1990). For more information in relation to the application of these ideas to working with young people, see *Dulwich Centre Newsletter*, 1995, Nos.2&3, on schooling and education.

12

Talking about men's violence, talking about prisons

Trying to talk about both men's violence and the issues of prisons can invite overwhelming reactions. These issues often touch our lives in profoundly powerful and personal ways. The effects of men's violence and the practices of power that enable us to imprison often create division - between men and women, between women, and between men. The following pages explore some of the complicated and heartfelt issues in relation to responding to men's violence in the hope of opening space for new conversations.

Largely as a result of the feminist movement, the hidden violence of our culture is slowly being named. Men's violence in the home, against women and children and against each other, is becoming less hidden and less accepted. At the same time, new forms of violence are being exposed. As Karlene Faith writes, *We don't yet know the full extent of child abuse ... research on elder abuse is still in its nascent stage, and the existence of cults which ritually torture and kill children is just beginning to surface* (1993, pp.98-99). Similarly, homophobic violence in our culture has only recently begun to be challenged, and its extent recognised. It seems a crucial time to be thinking about our responses to this violence. As issues like male sexual assault and violence within gay and lesbian relationships come more firmly into the light, more complex understandings of the relationships of power, gender, sexuality and violence are being considered. Perhaps these explorations will also spark conversations about notions of punishment and prisons.

In 1988, an Adelaide-based group of women organised what were named Women and Political Action Forums as a city-wide women's action group. A series of very successful forums were held, including one in which the group confronted the challenging issue of women's relationship to the state and the imprisonment of men in regard to violence against women. The forum was entitled *Protection or Punishment: Women, Power and the State. What is a Feminist Response to Male Violence? Do Fear, Safety and Prison Dominate our Thinking?* The following paper was prepared for that forum by the organising collective: Marg McHugh, Carol Johnston, Jo Hawke, and Suzanne Elliott. Eight years on, the questions it raises seem as relevant as ever.

Protection or punishment?

The theme of 'Protection or Punishment' was chosen by the organising collective because we wanted a chance to look at the ways in which women have sought to confront male violence over the past two decades. We hoped the Forum might provide a safe and supportive environment in which we could examine some of the difficulties and contradictions around this problem, particularly when we operate in a patriarchal or male-dominated society as well as one which is so clearly beset by class and racial inequalities.

The debate over protection for women covers many differing points of view - a fact which has been reinforced time and time again over the months that the organising collective met to plan for this Forum. We never had nor have we now reached a united perspective on this issue but we all have agreed that it is one of the most important and fundamental issues which confront women today.

The aim of this Forum, then, is to recognise from the outset that this is a contentious and often painful subject for women to talk about. We, the collective, have certainly experienced tense and potentially divisive exchanges on the issues while attempting to organise the Forum. Although these attempts have given us new insights into the issue, we all feel that our efforts at understanding have been worthwhile. So the ultimate aim of the Forum is simply to canvas the full spectrum of views on an issue which has at times divided the women's movement and at others united it. We also hope that we can take a step further in understanding the reasons behind women's continued suffering in a violent male-dominated society and find ways to break this cycle.

Before we open up the Forum as a 'speak-out', we felt that it could be useful to outline briefly the spectrum of debate covered by the organising collective. At one end of the spectrum, we felt that some feminists had argued that the state be responsible for male violence by increasing resources for policing, trials and lengthy periods of imprisonment. They have lobbied for the law to be revised to provide women with greater legal powers and credibility to prosecute men charged with crimes of violence against women, particularly for rape. This is to give greater legitimacy to crimes against women and hopes to ensure their safety. As a consequence, it also focuses on punishment of the perpetrators. This view relies on the existing state system to achieve protection for women.

At the other end of the spectrum, feminists have argued that using the existing state's means of social control and punishment guarantees further violence against women. By justifying the repressive nature of the police, courts and prisons, women sustain the values and practices of state control and punishment which is very inequitably applied. It is Black and working-class men that fill our prisons - yet we know that violence against women is wide-spread and cuts across these divisions of class and race in our society. Furthermore, the few violent men that are apprehended learn further brutality and sexist attitudes in jail.

In between these extreme positions are a multitude of other positions which we hope will be raised today and we believe that some of the major achievements of feminism should be acknowledged. Since the early 1970s, feminists have set up a large number of supportive services for women to help them escape from and avoid male violence. These have proved essential and, in many instances, life-saving measures for large numbers of women. They have also created inspiring and courageous networks of women who have been able to effect change in political attitudes and policy.

Feminism has always recognised the need to change the patriarchal base of our society, to change the social norms which influence male attitudes to women. Nevertheless, some feminists still maintain that male violence can only be addressed through a broader, community-based approach which does not recognise punishment as an effective tool of change but focuses on social conditions and education.

Despite our acknowledging the range of positions and attempting to analyse and decide on issues such as law and order, civil rights, punishment and the state, we often feel angry and powerless in dealing

with male violence. Our emotions are often at odds with our analysis.
Indeed, we sometimes feel quite different from the way we think we
should feel. Feminists have often been locked into either/or choices
about policy in relation to male violence and we may react to one issue
without recognising that it has a flow-on effect which is contradictory in
the long run, or if recognising the consequences we may feel powerless
to do anything about it.

After two decades of feminism, now is an opportune time to share
our collective thoughts on these issues in an effort to find new and
alternative responses to violence against women. On one thing the
collective was agreed, there is a fundamental contradiction in our desire
for safety and an over-reliance on the traditional responses of the state
to male violence. How do we, as feminists, want to build a less violent
society?

Men's responsibilities

Much of the thinking and action on alternative approaches to men's
violence in our community has been facilitated by women. Women have been
struggling with these issues publicly and privately for decades and longer, and
the previous piece articulates some of their dilemmas. In response to this
situation, I have written the following paragraphs as a man addressing other
men.

Exploring our responsibilities as men

Most violence in our culture is perpetrated by men. This violence is
widespread in our communities and there are very few men attempting to take
responsibility for addressing it. At the same time it is overwhelmingly men who
are incarcerated and men who work within prisons. What does this mean for us
as men who are wanting to create alternatives to the prison system?

How will we as men keep in our minds and spirits both the effects of
men's violence in our communities *and* the effects of prisons? How will we
ensure that the experiences of those who have survived men's violence are
respected in our conversations about prisons? Perhaps a first step will involve
being open about our dilemmas on these issues, the struggles we have in talking
with each other about men's violence, and how these issues touch our lives.

When talking about violence, how will we speak with one another in ways that do not split ourselves off from other men's violence, and that acknowledge our collective responsibilities? At the same time, how will we consider the power relations between men? How will we acknowledge the histories of racist violence, class-based domination, sexuality-based violence, and violence against young men?

When considering whether prison is an appropriate response to men's violence, the issues can become complicated. Although men's violence against women, children and other men occurs in all communities, our prisons are overwhelmingly filled with working-class men and Indigenous Australians. The violence of white middle-class men often remains invisible. Wealthy men often find alternative avenues open to them due to their access to resources, support, references and judicial prejudice. What different implications does this have for white middle-class Australian men, and those from working-class and Indigenous Australian communities?

For me, struggling with these issues has at times been overwhelming. I wonder how we will support each other as men in ways that allow us to be open to the effects of both men's violence and prisons? How will we support each other in ways that will be sustaining?

As men, and particularly as white middle-class men, I wonder how we will use our privilege to speak out about these issues in ways that do not replicate dominance and the silencing of women's voices? At the same time, how will we ensure that we don't simply remain silent either about prisons or about men's violence?

The idea of creating contexts in which we can share our struggles and dilemmas excites me. What other steps will we as men need to take in order to collectively, in partnership with women and other men, work towards radical alternatives to prison - radical alternatives that address men's violence?

Sharing our stories

Sheridan Linnell has worked for many years as a therapist and consultant with women and children who have experienced men's violence. Here she brings some of her struggles around these issues out into the light. After we spoke together in Adelaide, Sheridan wrote the following letter from the Blue Mountains, New South Wales, where she lives, and agreed to include it in this publication.

Thursday later afternoon
1st August 1996

Dear David,

Today started improbably blue and warm for a mountains August. Now the sky has whitened; the wind swings sharply in from the south, catapulting rain. I've fled the rollercoaster highway for the woody reassurance of my local cafe, where I'm writing you this letter.

When I met you in Adelaide recently, we shared with others a heartfelt wish that the injustices and brutalities of the prison system would end. That an ethics of accountability, a practice of community responsibility, can and will replace the class-ridden and racist politics and practices of imprisonment.

Just at this moment, though, that hope is dulled by the commonplace horrors of a typical working day. Travelling between mountains and plains, I listen to the stories of women and children, of young people, of families, whose lives have been torn by domestic violence and sexual abuse. I listen to the stories of the workers who work alongside these people. Heroic endurances, escapes, resistances and reclamations illuminate these tellings and retellings.

A worker describes her experience as a witness in court. How a lawyer systematically attempts to discredit her, to break her down professionally and personally through interrogation. Then offers her an 'out': perhaps the mother of the child has tricked the worker and set the child up, a campaign of revenge against the alleged perpetrator?

The worker steadfastly refuses these invitations. Nevertheless, it looks as though yet another child is about to be sentenced to regular and unsupervised access visits with the man she has identified as her abuser.

The process offers no opportunities for the worker to speak with this much maligned and now fearfully protective mother. But as the worker leaves the courtroom, the two women manage to exchange a smile. The lawyer's bullying tactics - which we subsequently identify as startlingly similar to the manipulations used by many perpetrators of child sexual abuse - have not cowed these women's spirits or sundered their alliance.

Few perpetrators are charged, fewer found guilty, rarely do they go to prison. Why are people convicted of break and enter, drug-related offences, car theft, far more likely to end up behind bars than a white, middle-class man who rapes his daughters and sons? Male violence is trivialised and isolated from the breadth of male culture, treated as *sickness or aberration, when to me it seems the logical pinnacle of the techniques of power exhibited by the lawyer in the courtroom. It is very difficult for me to relinquish images of punishment and retribution at the point where I am touched by the consequences of male violence.*

    I remind myself, then, who goes to prison. Who suffers most there. Those already subjugated and marginalised by dominant, white, middle-class culture. How prisons perpetuate the dispossession, demoralisation, torture and even murder, begun by my invading ancestors, of the traditional owners of this land.

    I remind myself, too, that I cannot, ever, speak for all women. That feminism too does not speak with a single voice. I thank some women from non-dominant cultures, especially some Indigenous women, whom I have worked alongside in the past, for this reminder. These women remind me of my responsibility to speak of and to my own, to beware exploiting my privilege as a white, 'upwardly mobile' woman.

    Other stories. A long day and night spent in a police cell with a handful of other women after being arrested in a demonstration. The threats, the 'minor' indignities, time frozen and windowless. How could anyone endure this for a month, a year, a lifetime?

    Looking back to this time I realise that somewhere I have crossed a line, been 'professionalised'. The police have become possible if difficult allies in the struggle against male violence; if I want to know the time I might just ask a policeman (or woman); rather than a force to be feared who might attack me for being a dirty lesbian.

    Another story. A dear friend's grief for a man she knew and loved, murdered behind prison walls. He was stabbed to death by another prisoner. My friend read this in the brutal anonymity of a newspaper report. She wept for him for a week. Working in the prisons, a connection deepened between her and this man, a 'lifer', although she never understood or excused his crimes of violence to women. She feared the judgements of other feminists who might see her as tricked or misguided. This deepened the isolation of her tearful vigil. One night we walked the foreshores under the moon, singing her goodbyes, her offerings of full blown flowers, gleaned from Glebe gardens, thrown to the stippled urban waters. How these flowers drifted insistently back to the shores, memories, questions, that refuse to go away.

    These memories, these questions, remember me into the company of people seeking alternatives to what is falsely named 'justice'. I have hopes that your consultations with Indigenous peoples here and overseas will map the ways. I fear that the dominant culture may depend too centrally on the politics of separation and subjugation for us to know how to form a circle. [see chapter 18]

In our talks, I remembered I had always objected to the incarceration of 'political prisoners'. And I realised that there is probably no-one in prison who is not a political prisoner.

Wishing you well,

Sheridan.

The dilemmas of how to respond

As a man working within prisons, I felt I was silent about men's violence on a daily basis - both the violence of the prison system and the violence of individual men with whom I was working. I often also 'turned a blind eye', or chose not to get more involved, in incidences of violence that were occurring within the prison.

Silences like mine about men's violence, and the perpetuation of violence that occurs within prisons, allow such scenarios to continue. At times I was profoundly out of my depth. I needed conversations about the complexities. I needed conversations that did not leap instantly to the enormous questions of large-scale alternatives, but instead conversations that explored ways of building communities and relationships with people who wished to find ways beyond. I longed for conversations that would challenge the ways in which I was participating with, and resisting, violent ways of being. I did little to seek out these conversations then, but I am searching now. Struggling with these issues in isolation often invited despair. Coming together across vastly different experiences, but all with some history of uncomfortableness or protest about prisons, as well as a determination to address men's violence, offers me hope and a chance to break the silence.

In this chapter I have attempted to explore the sorrow and the outrage of men's violence and the dilemmas in regard to the use of prisons as a response. I have tried to open up space for new ways of speaking about these issues - ways of speaking that may offer hope for the creation of partnerships and the possibilities for change.

13

Personal politics:
Becoming squarehead,
becoming gubba*

Most men and women within prison are incarcerated for *non*-violent crimes and overwhelmingly come from working-class and Indigenous Australian communities. As the injustices of the prison system have become clearer to me, so too have aspects of my life, my experience as a white, middle-class Australian. The following pages explore what it has meant for me to become more aware of my place within this culture. This chapter was written while I still worked within prisons.

Crossing boundaries

For the last three and a half years I have made the journey from my white middle-class home in inner-city Sydney to work within a men's maximum security prison. When I first stepped up to the metallic gates of the

---

* This chapter has already appeared in *Bedtime Stories for Tired Therapists* (1995), Leela Anderson (ed). Dulwich Centre Publications' editors decided to include it in both books because it was felt that it made an important contribution to the different themes of each publication. Leela Anderson's book focuses on the personal dilemmas of individual therapists as they seek to come to terms with their work. As this chapter raises issues of class, race, and the politics of professional practice, it was felt to be too important to leave out. Similarly, it forms an essential part of this current book, because it outlines the author's personal history and involvement in prison work.

prison in which I work I was overwhelmed by the structure itself. Rarely, if ever, have I felt so small, so insignificant. There was also a strong sense of history, as if the sandstone walls were harbouring secrets. I know now that various Koori inmates and workers experience the spirits of various parts of the prisons. Where possible, those who are housed in what were once the cells of the condemned, burn oils to free the souls.

The wind is always howling across the bay on which the prison is built. Before I move from one world to the next I always take a slightly deeper breath than usual and try to hold the colours of the outside world in my mind. Having stepped up to the wall I would ring the buzzer and after the obligatory wait, the grey solid steel gate in front of me opens. I grunt a 'G'day' as I ruffle through my wallet until I find my ID. Having flashed it coolly and received a nod of recognition for my efforts, I walk on through.

I notice that my posture has changed. My shoulders are back slightly further than usual, there's a tightness across my neck, and I've hidden every sign of effeminacy from my walk. It's the same posture I held on the football field all those years ago. Even my voice is different, lower somehow, more laid-back and my language full of 'mate' and a litany of adjectives that I've only come to use since working inside.

Unfortunately the work shifts move the prison officers around so much that I rarely know the officer on the gate by name. It would make a significant difference if I did, and I tell myself that I must make a greater effort. While waiting, always waiting, for the next set of gates to be opened, the same stale air greets my face. On my tongue it feels like it's been through everyone's cigaretted lungs before it has got to me. Finally the gate swings open, I walk through and it closes behind me. I am back inside.

I stride through the centre of the prison, the 'circle', and there, as always, I find sweet relief. For every story of sorrow in prison there is a story of triumph of spirit. Meticulously painted on the front of each cell block are huge murals. No place is uglier than prison, no art more beautiful than these murals. Amongst the grey and the desolate, in the least expected of places, there is always beauty, resistance and life.

Becoming squarehead

Inherited privilege, and the assumption of it, is something one carries in one's very bones. (Penelope 1994, p.54)

Working in prisons has meant coming in contact with communities that are not my own. To find myself teaching a welfare/sociology class to long-termers in a maximum security prison was to find myself transported into a culture very different from the white middle-class world to which I am accustomed. One morning I naively asked the group what they would have called me had we met as children. Without a moment's hesitation, and with a dead-pan expression, one guy replied, 'A squarehead'. Unfazed, I asked what this meant and with a large grin he explained, 'A stuck-up poof who can't fuck'. My lessons had begun. Far from sounding like an insult (or a challenge to explore issues of sexuality or homophobia), it seemed a generous, if rather blunt, invitation to explore our differences and my privilege.

At this stage, in hysterics and with laughter filling the room, I managed to articulate that I would have thought of them as 'westies' (from the western suburbs), but that I wouldn't have dared call them this to their faces, as I would have been terrified of being beaten up by the violent, ugly and stupid young men that I believed they were!

Believe it or not, this was the beginning of ongoing attempts to build partnerships across a class divide. Their naming of my middle-class experience challenged me to explore and articulate what it means to be middle-class. It was the beginning of an ongoing process of rewriting and understanding my life through the experiences of working-class people. It is this process that I refer to as 'becoming squarehead'.

What does it mean to be middle-class?

One of the first things that was absolutely clear was that they were much more familiar with the term 'westie' than I was with the term 'squarehead'. To be middle-class means that one's culture is rarely the 'object' of analysis. We 'professionals' too often maintain our invisible privilege or our privilege of invisibility. In this way we avoid acknowledging how we have benefited from class relations and instead blame those who are disadvantaged by such relations for resisting. Everyday in prisons 'professionals' such as myself deny the impact of class relations by mystifying the process of imprisonment, by calling prisons 'correctional centres', by claiming that self-harm is 'manipulative', by diagnosing those who challenge professional practices as 'difficult' and unworthy of 'help', and by understanding crimes as caused by individual pathology.

For me, being a middle-class 'professional' meant I assumed that I could develop a curriculum and deliver it in my language. Somehow my university degree was supposed to give me the credentials to judge and assess others and their work. These were the skills for which I was employed, the reason why I was to be paid. It is a part of middle-class experience to assume that 'professional' skills are valuable to those with whom we work. Often we 'professionals' can participate in practices of power and domination, all the while keeping our assumptions, privilege and cultural motivations hidden.

When I was named 'squarehead', however, my privilege was challenged. I was no longer 'normal' in a middle-class world, I was a 'squarehead' in a 'westies' world. It was me who used a different language, wore different clothes, held different values. I've never done time, I have no tattoos, don't know how to read a form guide, don't smoke, indeed I'm asthmatic. I don't do weights and I don't even play a sport any more. When different guys constantly asked me how I had made the corners on my wooden briefcase I had to respond that my last woodworking attempt was in Year 9 when I inadvertently created a triangular car.

A squarehead reflects

By naming me as squarehead, the men with whom I work were inviting me to acknowledge the ways in which I have benefited from class relations, and to realise that they had often been on the other end of these dynamics. They were demanding of me that I resist the common middle-class assumption that people in prison are in some way more racist, dominating and/or sexist than those not in prison. There is no doubt that prisons breed violence, racism and sexism, but when people enter them they are likely to be doing so because they have less money and/or darker skin than others, rather than because of some deficiency or oppressive characteristic. The most invigorating, open and honest discussions I have ever had with men about gender and sexual violence have occurred in prisons, while the most difficult, frustrating and crazy-making conversations have occurred with middle-class men such as myself who profess to be 'pro-feminist'.

Becoming squarehead has similarly altered my views on crime. Where once my view of crime involved stereotypical views of working-class men committing property offences or street crimes, now the first thing that flashes into my mind is the crime that is prison. I think of the crime that we middle-class Australians commit by allowing those who live in poverty to be criminalised and brutalised. I realise now that the use of prisons does not reduce violence but instead both creates it and moves it around so that it occurs behind prison walls, between working-class people. It was a further shock to my squarehead consciousness to discover that many people who commit armed robberies understand their actions through sophisticated analyses of capitalism, and that some are knowledgeable of whole histories of which I am completely unaware, histories of worker and prison movements.

Perhaps more profound, however, has been recognising the specific practices or emphases of my middle-class culture, how they differ from working-class cultures and the effects of these differences. The very conversation that began my process of becoming squarehead would never have occurred in the adult middle-class culture from which I come. The directness, honesty, and the burly sense of humour that were essential to challenge my middle-class experience are important aspects of working-class cultures. The emphasis on politeness and reserve that characterises my middle-class culture profoundly supports the maintenance of the status quo. Whenever a member of an oppressed group expresses their outrage, their claims can be disregarded simply because they are not expressed in middle-class 'adult' ways.

Christian McEwen describes middle-class 'niceness' as camouflage:

> *Upper-class betterness is built on centuries of other people's work. It is built on land and industry maintained by other people, income and profits got at their expense. Most of those involved are well aware of this, and the feelings (understandably) are strong. Guilt and fear and ignorance on the part of those in power, anger and resentment on the part of the workers, threaten to burst forth at any minute. Under the circumstances, niceness is a very useful tool. It gives the upper-classes some sort of camouflage to operate behind, at the same time as it aims to distract everyone from what is actually going on.* (1994, p.271)

These challenges have meant coming to terms with the fact that the entire view of professionalism in which I had been enculturated is at best irrelevant, and at worst offensive, to those with whom I work. It has meant recognising that teaching is a two-way process, except initially when the only person learning was me! It has meant recognising that the only ways in which I can be effective within a culture that is not my own is to build relations of trust (see chapter 14).

Retracing histories

Becoming squarehead has not only revealed to me oppressive 'professional' practices, but it has also opened up new ways of understanding aspects of my life. Incidents I once viewed as 'normal' I now see as products of privilege. Middle-class privilege meant that the values being espoused at my school were not in conflict with those of my family. It meant never hearing conversations about money for the entirety of my childhood. One of the reasons I can write this article is because middle-class privilege has allowed me to be comfortable with the written word, with academia. Being middle-class let me see police as people who would protect me rather than assault me. It meant that my family was never intruded upon by the state, and that therefore the only institution I had to deal with as a child was school.

Perhaps most importantly, middle-class privilege has meant having the opportunity to become rich and powerful. So saturated with opportunities was my childhood that when I received a high-school matriculation mark that enabled me to study medicine or law, this represented to me not an opportunity but more of the same competitive scramble.

At the same time, becoming squarehead has revealed to me the influences of a working-class history on one side of my family that has been hidden and silenced. The pressure to appear middle-class and the benefits for doing so must have outweighed, for my grandparents, the value of maintaining their connection to working-class culture. How impossibly difficult it must be to move from a westie world into a world of squareheads! Whether my family notices it or not our working-class history lives on in the generosity of my cousins who, even in times of great hardship, prioritise the giving of gifts. It lives on through my father and his familiar cry of 'Life is too short', the ways in which he lives day by day and his attitude to money. I see now that my mother's request to 'keep your options open' is born out of a different, middle-class tradition. I see how her astute planning and distribution of family resources derives in some ways from generations of having the option and privilege to save and accumulate. I see how my respect and passion for education, books and knowledge have been nurtured by a middle-class culture. I feel that my life has been greatly enriched by both traditions.

I wonder if the challenges of those with whom I work influence me in the ways that they do because they resonate with my (hidden) family histories. I recognised only while writing this article that on one side of my family a great grandfather was a working-class man who spent time imprisoned, while on the other side a great-great-grandfather was the first Chief Justice of Australia who imprisoned others.

Despite the mixed heritage, it is clear to me and to those with whom I work that I am a squarehead. Becoming aware of this has changed the person that I am. It has opened new landscapes for me to explore, new histories and new futures. The men who originally challenged me have moved on now, transported to other prisons, but their laughter and words remain with me. I wonder if our interactions offered them as much as they did me. If not, the injustice in some ways continued.

Becoming Gubba

Across the country there are many different Indigenous Australian words to describe non-Indigenous people, including *gubs, gubbas, murantawi, balanda* and *gadiya* (Egan, in Graham 1994, p.77). As I am from New South Wales, my interactions have largely been with Koori people who know me, and describe me, as a gubba. Using the language of other peoples can be problematic and perpetuate acts of colonisation. I hope in this instance, however, that my use of the word gubba opens up space for me and others to consider what it means to be white in ways that encourage the challenging of racism and white supremacy in this country.

It is a reflection on race relations in this culture, that it wasn't until I worked behind bars that I had any meaningful contact with Indigenous Australian culture or people. Todd Gordon was the first person to tell me that I was, in his language, a gubba - a white person. More recently I became aware that the word gubba is derived from the word government. It seems a particularly useful word to locate our history as white Australians in relation to the State, to the police, to prisons and to the invasion of this country. Seeing myself through a different language was once again the beginning of a process of rewriting and understanding my life, this time through the experiences of Indigenous Australians. It is this process that I refer to as 'becoming gubba'.

The events of one afternoon further shifted the ground under my feet. I had been invited by a number of Koori men, with whom I had been working, to sit in on a planning meeting for an upcoming Koori project. I was the only gubba present and also the only prison employee. As the conversation took a particular tack, I began to express my concerns about particular decisions that looked as if they were soon to be made. After further discussion, a number of men in the group began to get very agitated with me, until finally it was suggested in no uncertain terms that I leave the room.

As I walked out I realised that I had violated the sacredness of the invitation that I had received. I had spoken in a space in which I had no right to speak. It was the first time that I realised that there were places and times in which my skin colour, my ancestry, my privilege meant that it was oppressive for me to speak. As a white person I had believed this land was mine to travel and speak in wherever I chose. Becoming gubba has meant, and continues to mean, recognising that I have responsibilities concerning how, when and where I travel, speak and act. That afternoon also taught me a further important lesson. Having recognised the ways in which I had inadvertently replicated white supremacy, I wrote a letter to the group and dialogue was maintained. The generosity of the Indigenous Australian men involved made it clear to me that being yelled at was an invitation to challenge the ways I was relating, not a demand for our relationships to end.

What does it mean to be white?

Exploring what it means to be gubba is only one aspect of many necessary for me to truly examine what it means to be white and to challenge racism. The following pages do not in any detail attempt to struggle with how I as a white Australian participate in racist practices towards other immigrants to this country. Obviously these issues are of great importance. Problematising what it means to be gubba is a starting point for me to explorations of race and racism.

Being white has meant that I haven't had to think or feel about issues of racism until well into my twenties. I have had the privilege of not noticing my own skin colour. White privilege has meant that I have been able to live in a land conquered by my ancestors and ignore the implications. It has meant that I can go shopping without feeling as if everyone is looking at me in case I may shop-lift. White supremacy has meant that I have been able to take for granted that I belong here simply because I belong nowhere else. It has meant not noticing the irony that white racism has caused those whose home this country has been for tens of thousands of years to often feel excluded and unwelcome.

Fundamentally, to be white in Australia has meant denying that I am a gubba. It has meant denying that there is any process I need to go through, any work I need to do in relation to the place that I find myself, the actions of my ancestors and the racism that continues today. Being white has meant being able to claim that we can look only at the present and the future, that to take history seriously is to 'look backwards' and brings only 'guilt'.

It seems to me that the Indigenous Australian men with whom I was working were challenging these views. They were challenging me to see myself not as simply 'normal', or as generically 'Australian' but specifically as gubba. They were challenging my comfortableness, my privilege, and at the same time inviting me to develop a greater understanding of my place here.

For me, listening to Indigenous Australians' stories of this country's history, the stories that have been for so long silenced, is a first step. I have to consciously allow myself to be affected by these stories, to stop myself from disconnecting from them. I have had to recognise that those who did the killing were doing so on behalf of people like me. They believed that their actions were connected to us, even if we try to disconnect ourselves from them. As Duncan Graham writes:

> *We are the recipients of stolen goods. The men who cleared the land of trees and rocks to grow crops and graze stock also cleared the land of its owners and users. Those invaders said they demolished and destroyed and killed for the sake of future generations. We are all part of that future planned by others. Like you, my family and I find shelter, warmth, profit, security, pleasure, comfort and joy from living on the proceeds of thieves and killers.* (1994, p.107)

Becoming gubba for me does not mean viewing shame as an end to be avoided but rather a part, along with exhilaration, sadness and joy, of coming to terms with the histories of this country and its ongoing racism, honouring the experiences of Indigenous Australians and finding ways to move forwards. For me the connection to history comes also through my direct family relations. My great-great-grandfather sent many Indigenous Australians to their deaths as a judge and ignored their rights wholeheartedly in the constitution which he played a part in constructing. My great-great-uncles killed many Indigenous Australians in the process of claiming land in Queensland. I was never aware of these connections until very recently. One generally has to search to hear of how one's family has contributed to the genocide of Indigenous Australians. Of course, such contributions to genocide are not over, they are continuing.

Becoming gubba for me not only involves a new relationship to the histories of this country but also recognising the legacies of these histories, and the ways we perpetuate them. For instance when I began work in the prison system I was most frightened of the darkest-skinned men and therefore was less likely to offer them my services or hear their stories. Similarly, the group I work for, Men Against Sexual Assault (Sydney), has perpetuated the silence that surrounds histories of sexual assault in this country. We have ignored the fact that the men who we read about in history books, the pioneers, explorers, politicians, statesmen were also the men who raped Indigenous women and forced the offspring of these assaults to live on reserves. We have ignored the history of sexual assault on missions, in homesteads and in boys' homes.

As Victor Lewis states in the film *The Color of Fear* (Stir-Fry Productions 1991), the most toxic, lethal racism is perpetuated by 'very nice folks' who would claim they are against injustice. This rings true in my life as I am confronted with the ways I am blind to racist beliefs and practices.

Even the ways in which I think are within white supremacist frameworks. The highly mechanistic metaphors which we use in white-Anglo culture to understand ourselves and our relationships have only become obvious to me through their comparison with the metaphors of Koori culture. I recall listening to Vicky Barrett when she was to present to white teachers on issues of Indigenous Australian culture. She described a feeling of pain in her stomach which she understood as a metaphor of pregnancy. She hoped the session was to give birth to new ways of understanding. The contrast between Indigenous Australian ways and speaking to the world of academia, in which one tries to assert one's 'objective facts' over others, is apparent. Being invited into these other ways of viewing life has been a thoroughly enriching experience. At the same time it has shown me glimpses of the myriad of ways in which race and culture are a part of the very air we breathe and how challenging white supremacy involves noticing what we gubbas seldom notice.

Retracing histories

Becoming gubba is also involving retracing entire histories of my life and seeing them through different lenses. Some of my earliest memories involve playfully exploring the mountain behind our suburban Canberra house. I guess it was a hill really, cleared for grazing. I suppose now that once this land was occupied by the Ngarigo people but by the time my small feet were traipsing (trespassing) amongst the rocks and dried grass there was no sign of their earlier explorations - or at least to my untrained five-year-old eyes. My relationship to these memories is now changed as part of the process of becoming gubba. It is hard to describe how, but my sense of place is altered by knowing that other people's feet had explored 'my mountain' for thousands of years. To discover that the Black Mountain where we used to picnic was once Blacks' Mountain, or that the turrets on country houses were built for the express purpose of shooting Indigenous Australians, alters my entire perception of myself and my country.

Never when at school did I have to think of myself as white, only that others were 'not white'. Constantly I would define others, with the support of white supremacist culture, in relation to my colour, my place, my culture. Looking back I realise now that the boys who were called 'boonga' must have been Indigenous Australians. At the time, so whitewashed was our school and my background that I didn't even make the connection. Another boy in my year was referred to as 'nip', another constantly taunted rather than praised for his soccer skills and Greek background, and 'Jew' was a generic insult.

I did nothing to either enquire as to the origin of these nick-names or to try to stop these racial divisions or slurs. From the make-up of the student and teacher populations, to the language used and history taught, my school was a white school. And me? I was simply Australian and normal - the subject of no taunts. The language we spoke was mine, the sports we played the same that my father played.

Even my understandings of my teenage years are altered by hearing the stories of Indigenous Australians. The nihilism and emptiness of my adolescence that I have analysed through theories of gender and youth powerlessness, I now also understand as a product of white ways. The individualism and competitiveness that I have often called 'capitalism' or 'dominant masculinity' perhaps I should call 'white people's ways'.

Cultural histories

Understanding what it means to be white is also involving tracing the histories of my ancestors, for there one can find meanings upon which to build. My Anglicised name was invented just prior to the Second World War, changed from van den Bergh, a Dutch name, in order that our family not be confused with the Afrikaaners in South Africa who were supporting Hitler. My grandfather who had Flemish and Dutch ancestry later become a British Israelite, believing that the British were the lost ten tribes of Israel. Somewhere along the line, mainly due to British imperialism, we lost all connection to our Dutch heritage. My white privilege and my middle-class status converge in this story in that my grandfather and grandmother, both from working-class families, moved from England to become privileged whites in the newly conquered Rhodesia (now Zimbabwe). The change of status probably enabled my father to meet my wealthy Australian mother years later in England. My very existence is therefore tied up in the colonisation of Africa.

When I trace the histories of Anglo culture it is clear that its dominant stories dictate a competitive, individualistic way of seeing the world, a spirituality of a hierarchical judgemental God and a concept of community based around 'the family' and the rule of the father. My blood-lines encourage conquering, using (or now saving) the environment, rather than seeing ourselves and the earth as in intricate relationship.

But no culture is monolithic. Even within cultures of imperialist history there are a multitude of myths, meanings and traditions. Searching my ancestries for alternative cultural meanings on which to build excites me. On a cultural scale, there are English traditions of the rebels of seventeenth century England, the democratic communitarians and libertarians who were suppressed by Cromwell and King alike. As Christine Dann writes, we can choose the traditions we wish to build upon: *Winstanley and the suffragettes, whom I saw condemned in Lloyd George's handwriting in the British museum, were and are my people, the Britons I want to claim as ancestors* (in King 1991, p.51).

In my own life I am revelling in unearthing histories of spirituality connected to the earth and justice and I am constantly in wonder at the written word. These land-scapes are part of my cultural tradition of which I am proud. Other threads of cultural tapestry await me as I trace our Dutch, Scottish and Welsh traditions. In relation to my family histories, I can see that within my ancestors' lives there were many threads that show their dedication to justice. Furthermore, I know that much of their lives went into trying to create a better world for future generations - including me.

My identity as an Australian

More important than tracing the histories of my ancestors, however, is the process of here and now. Becoming gubba has involved the recognition that Indigenous Australians understand far more about my people than we do about them, and perhaps even more than we know about ourselves.

Through resisting coming to terms with being white, perhaps we have not come to terms with our own place in this country. If we as gubbas take up the invitations from the Indigenous peoples of this land to come to terms with our histories and our ongoing racism then it seems there will be hope for the development of truly Australian identities for non-Indigenous people - identities based on justice.

> *... white Australian terra nullius attitude right from the beginning of early settlement* [sic] *has led, I believe, to a spiritual numbness, Judith Wright's 'sightless shadow' at the centre of the national psyche.* (Scott, in King 1991, p.181)

Perhaps we have an opportunity to rid ourselves of this spiritual numbness and perhaps part of this process would involve acknowledging that much of what we refer to as Australian culture, when we mean white Australian culture, exists because of our relationship with the Indigenous peoples of this land. Ted Egan writes:

> *'She'll be right' is an outlook we all like to think is 'typically Australian'. Well believe me, whether we like to acknowledge it or not, we have inherited this laconic approach to life from the first Australians.* (in Graham 1994, p.74)

Similarly parts of Australia's social landscape are due to the efforts of Aboriginal activism. The establishment of community legal and health centres and prison reforms are just a few examples of where Indigenous Australian reforms have gone on to inspire changes that have benefitted all Australians (Baker 1993).

Hopefully, coming to terms with the fact that we are the products of imperialism would also mean that we would demand an end to Australia's ongoing support of imperialism, be it in Bougainville or East Timor, through selling uranium to the French, or allowing US bases on our soil.

Perhaps it would begin further processes of challenging racism. Becoming gubba is obviously not enough. White Australians such as myself are not racist only towards Indigenous Australians. The complexities involved in exploring how becoming gubba fits with challenging the racism we direct at other new arrivals to this country certainly need to be considered. For me, tapping into the histories of my people and the affects we have had on the Indigenous peoples of this country in some way locates me, names my experience. I hope this will create possibilities to further challenge the ways I participate in white supremacist practices.

Escape from prison history

> *Between convict and black, much blood is mingled in the soil of this ... island.* (Hughes 1988, p.120)

In order to come to terms with white peoples' crimes of the past against the Indigenous peoples of this country perhaps we will need to come to terms with ways of addressing wrongs that are not simply based on vengeance and punishment. As earlier chapters have described, this country was invaded so that it could be turned into a prison - a place where the working-class of Britain could be punished and hidden. Traditions of punishment, incarceration and vengeance still dominate our approaches to 'righting wrongs'.

It is of little surprise that in this context we white Australians do not want to admit to the wrongs carried out in our names. To take such responsibility, in our way of thinking, leads only to retribution and guilt. And when the crime is genocide there is all the more reason for denial. Indigenous Australians, however, seem to be attempting to show us that there are other ways forward - restorative ways, reconciliation. In the process perhaps we will realise that the ways in which we address crime in this country have far more to do with perpetuating race and class injustice than anything else.

It is no coincidence, in my mind, that white imperialism began in this country through the use of prison, that prisons are now a cornerstone in the continuing oppression of Indigenous Australians, and that the issue of punishment and vengeance needs to be addressed if we are ever to come to terms with our histories.

Towards the future

Working in prisons means I now witness injustice that once I did not see. It is a part of privilege to have the option to be cocooned from the results of injustice, including poverty and incarceration. Being a witness brings further responsibilities: to reach out to my own kind, my people.

Finding ways to talk with other gubbas, other squareheads, finding ways to support each other in facing the challenges of confronting racism and middle-class privilege will, perhaps, be starting-points. How we manage to resist trying to stand apart from other white people, other middle-class people, how we resist being more 'anti-racist than thou' will probably be a measure of our commitment. As Chris McLean writes (in another context):

> *There are often very few opportunities for people to learn about these issues, and if we have had such opportunities, it is itself the result of privilege, and does not place us outside of our own culture.* (1995, p.7)

The processes of becoming squarehead, becoming gubba, are seeking to challenge white privilege and middle-class privilege. As a middle-class person, as a member of a colonising race, the only way for me to know the usefulness of these explorations is to be open to the feedback of Indigenous Australians and working-class people. If we are ever to work in meaningful partnership across race and class divides then perhaps we, as white middle-class professionals, will need to be willing to listen to what those with whom we work really think of us and to create the spaces in which to hear.

Where once my life was consumed and emptied by the constant competition and isolation that is necessary to maintain privilege, now it is enriched by the sharing of stories, and the search for ways to resist. The challenges of those with whom I work have opened up new ways for me to understand my life. Entire histories and landscapes that were once invisible are now available for me to draw upon.

The conversations, friendships and relationships that have been a part of my life behind prison walls have greatly shaped the person I now am. I hope these processes will continue. I hope they lead to action. From me, and others like me, I hope they lead to acts of redress. And together, across differences, I hope they lead to acts of creation - the creation of new histories and new futures.

PART THREE

Beyond the Prison

Reached a new day, through old ways, we'll return.
Reached a new day, through old ways, we'll learn.
'Our Home, Our Land', Lou Bennett, 1995.

There are cracks appearing in the culture of imprisonment. Both within and beyond prison walls there is work occurring that opens possibilities for great change. This section seeks to trace these developments. Out of the communities most affected by imprisonment are being born alternative responses to crime and violence. By no means are they simply 'easy options' for offenders, for the communities most affected by imprisonment are also those most affected by crime. The work of the Community Justice Centre in Harlem describes moving from notions of rehabilitation to community building, developing meaningful forms of reconciliation between offenders and their communities, and finding ways to make prison systems accountable to the communities most affected by their operation.

This section also describes the work of Clint Deveaux, a judge in Atlanta, Georgia, USA, and the changes that he is bringing about in relation to ways in which to view the courtroom. Finally, the focus moves to Indigenous communities in Canada, in Aotearoa/New Zealand, and here in Australia.

These communities are claiming back the right to address issues of crime and violence in their own ways. In the process they are lighting paths for all of us to follow.

But first, having earlier discussed the imprisoning effects of some of the practices of of psychology and education, the following chapter explores the development of alternative practices in these realms within prisons.

14

Beyond
imprisoning psychology

This chapter is in three parts and describes examples of work by 'professionals' within the prison system. While dedicating a chapter to the work of professionals, I am conscious that most exciting work within prisons and beyond is carried out not by professionals but instead by prisoners and/or ex-prisoners. I am aware of the ways in which we professionals are often complicit with the running of institutions of degradation, and the ways in which professional culture often restricts us from contributing to radical change. This chapter will touch upon these issues, and the rest of this book explores the work which has emerged from the communities most affected by imprisonment, and which is being done by current and ex-prisoners.

Many prisoners would see most professionals working within prisons as complicit with the system, despite perhaps having the best of intentions. While reading the descriptions of work facilitated by professionals such as myself, it may be useful to keep in mind the following questions:

- What are the responsibilities of workers within the prison system to find ways of speaking out about the injustices they witness?
- What are the political implications of being paid by institutions and departments that degrade and dehumanise?
- How can one remain working within prisons without becoming accustomed or acclimatised to the daily injustices?

In many ways during my time as a worker within the prison system I was complicit in the operation of institutions of degradation. I was paid by the

Department of Corrective Services. I saw things that I did not speak up about for fear of losing my job, for fear of facing the wrath of the superintendent (again) and out of a sense of isolation and hopelessness. I hope this book can play some part in assisting those who are currently working within prisons to feel less alone and more empowered to take action.

As professionals, it is crucial that we develop ways of working that open the possibilities for radical change rather than closing them down. This chapter explores ways of working that may play a part in moving beyond prisons.

What doesn't work

David Roskin (not his real name) is a prisoner within an Australian medium security prison. At age seven a psychiatrist 'diagnosed' that he had a problem with females in authority and recommended counselling. Over the next seventeen years he saw over a hundred different psychologists and psychiatrists. He describes his experiences of psychology and offers ten clear recommendations for those working within prisons:

If it wasn't my fault, it was my family's fault. They looked for places to label and blame rather than to treat. Psychologists that I have seen have spent a great deal of their time attempting to quantify or label me rather than help me. I have been diagnosed as a multi-personality disorder on two separate occasions, paranoid schizophrenic, borderline personality disorder, psychopath, sociopath, psychotic, manic-depressive and a thousand other terms that I can't remember.

They have attempted to place me in chemical straight-jackets. They've also tried physical restraints, sensory deprivation - they locked me in a room with nothing as a treatment - they've tried hypnotism, meditation, word association, inkblots, good thought therapy (when you had a good thought you had to put a little coloured dot on a piece of paper!), general counselling/listening, writing tasks, a few foods diet. I've been under a Freudian, Jungian, even 'deconstructionalism' therapy where you had to look at a cup, and think of the thoughts behind the thoughts, tear down the original thoughts into splinters and make coherent thoughts of this, like what the cup is made out of. They've tested me with MMPIs, IQ tests, psych tests, WAIS-R tests, standard non-societal-affected matrices test, spatial tests ...

They have attempted to place themselves in a position of authority towards me and I always let them. I've learnt to use my brain. To challenge their world would be far more destructive for me. The reports that came out whenever I did were not as nice. I can't honestly say that any of them helped. There are things however that psychs could do that would be useful:

Ten recommendations for psychologists in prisons

(i) *Recognise firstly that you can't out-think the one who is being counselled.*

(ii) *Lay down specific objectives, once you understand what's going on, as a joining thing.*

(iii) *Don't come up with clever ideas. The person's best cure is usually themselves.*

(iv) *I recognise the need in extreme circumstances for medication, as rarely as possible. Medication alters the way people perceive reality so the answers they can give for themselves are altered. They don't provide a true reflection as to the problems or the actual state of mind.*

(v) *Ignore most types of therapies and instead concentrate on just understanding the person without the labels and possible causes, but understanding where that person is right now and seek to establish a path that is beneficial to them in the future.*

(vi) *Establish procedures in which follow-up counselling can be realistically done. If the person is here for two days and then moves to another jail the person may slip between the cracks.*

(vii) *Seek to establish some sort of stable atmosphere. If appropriate, try to arrange suitable employment for the inmate, some sort of focus for self-worth.*

(viii) *Don't necessarily believe that you have the right answers.*

(ix) *Don't be afraid to ask questions. They always asked all sorts of questions but never the relevant ones. They were paranoid about upsetting me. You can't help a person if you don't know what's wrong with them.*

(x) *Time needs to be more flexible. Insufficient time is spent, an hour a week in jail is not sufficient.*

The following three examples of work resonate, to my mind, with David Roskin's principles. The first is occurring within a detention centre for young people in Ottawa, Canada, and involves assisting young people to reclaim their lives from crime and drugs. The second is concerned with creating the context for those within prison to reclaim stories about themselves that the prison culture denies. And the third involves attempts to build community support within the yards of a maximum security prison.

A. Externalising 'crime' and 'drugs'

Mishka Lysack is a therapist within a detention centre in Ottawa, Canada. There he is involved in trying to assist young men and women to identify what they want in their lives, and to reconnect with their own knowledges and strengths. The work described below builds upon the understandings and work of Michael White and David Epston (1990). Inviting the young people to step out of seeing themselves as 'wholly criminal, bad or as young offenders' is often a first step.

As David Roskin clearly articulated above, our culture, and constructions of psychology in particular, encourage people to think of problems as internal, as a part of their own character. Within prisons this is particularly true. As described in chapter 1, a profound consequence of prison culture is that those incarcerated constantly evaluate their lives, motivations and weaknesses. Prison culture encourages those who have committed a crime to identify as a criminal, as an inmate, as an offender prone to committing further crime. Such an understanding is often self-perpetuating and limits possibilities for action: *If you are the problem, then there's not much you can do about it - except maybe act against yourself* (*Dulwich Centre Newsletter*, 1995, No.1, pp.18-19).

'Externalising conversations' are ways of talking about problems that make it possible for people to experience an identity that is distinct or separate from the problem. Through the use of externalising conversations the young women and men in the Ottawa detention centre are invited to articulate the problems on which they wish to work. The two most common problems are those of crime and drugs.

Mishka Lysack invites these young men and women to talk about the effects of crime and/or drugs on their lives and relationships in ways that create space for them to separate themselves from these problems. As he describes:

> *The more specific the cartography of the territory of the problem's influence in the young person's life, and the more detailed the exposé of the attitudes and the tactics which the problem such as 'Crime' or 'Drugs' uses to gain the upper hand in a young person's life, the better idea we have of how one might regain control of one's life.* (Lysack, 1996, p.5)

Steve[1] and Mishka talking about drugs and crime

The following transcript is an example of a conversation between Mishka and Steve, in which the attitudes and tactics of the problem, in this case drugs, are exposed, and the effects of drugs upon Steve's life and the lives of others are documented. This creates space for Steve to begin to separate himself from drugs and crime.

Mishka: *I'm hearing a common thread: are there some attitudes which Drugs enlisted you into?*

Steve: *I don't know what you mean.*

Mishka: *Like, some bad attitudes, or a kind of outlook on life?*

Steve: *It gives me a negative outlook. like I think they're all against me.*

Mishka: *Okay, that's one example; what other kinds of bad attitudes did you get recruited into?*

Steve: *My anger got a lot worse. If I didn't get what I wanted, I'd punch a hole in the wall.*

Mishka: *I can hear two attitudes here: 'I should get what I want ...'*

Steve: *Yeah.*

Mishka: *And 'If I don't get what I want ...' how did you express that?*

Steve: *... just take out my anger on walls.*

Mishka: *Any other attitudes? You mentioned earlier about only going to your family for meals?*

Steve: *I kind of just used them; they're only good for stuff I can get. But when I was straight, I wasn't like that and I did care. But I had a different way of doing it. I wasn't good at showing my feelings.*

Mishka: *So another attitude would be 'Don't show you care or share your feelings'.*

Steve: *It put me in an attitude, like if no one cares for me, I won't care for them. I'm alone. It's me against the world.*

Mishka: [Writing] *'Everyone is against me.' And 'I don't care about anyone else.' Wow, that's quite a list. Can you think of any others?*

Steve: *No, I can't think of any.*

Mishka: *As you got recruited into these bad attitudes, did it lead to bad habits, like ... how you found yourself treating people?*

Steve: *I became more aggressive, lots of threats, ... and spent more time with the wrong people. Hang out with lots of dealers.*

Mishka: *How does Drugs convince you into these attitudes? Do you just fall into them?*

Steve: *You don't notice it at the time ... you can't see how you're falling into a certain pattern. Different drugs do different things. Hash makes me lazy. But coke got me to do lots of crime to support my habit.*

Mishka: *All these attitudes: Why do they bother you? In what way are they going against what you really want for your life?*

Steve: *People put on a show or mask. I was falling into that category: popular with lots of money. I was like two different people.*

Mishka: *Which do you prefer?*

Steve: *Positive; the other one's a waste of time.*

Mishka: *It sounds like Drugs ... manipulates you?*

Steve: *Yeah, it glamorises crime.*

Steve also speaks clearly about the ways crime and drugs encouraged him to view himself as 'criminal', as a 'drug addict', and how this made it more difficult to overcome these problems:

Mishka: *So this becomes the truth of who you are, like I'm a ... what does this look like in your life? Like I'm a negative person ...?*

Steve: *I'm a criminal, I'm a drug addict.*

Mishka: *And as you buy into that, does that tighten its grip even more, extend the power of drugs ...?*

Steve: *Yeah, in some ways.*

Mishka: *How do you think? How does it do this?*

Steve: *Because it's more influential on your* mind [gestures with his fist in his hand]. *You go to that state and truly believe that that's what you are and all you ever will be. It helps that other*

> *people are saying 'That's all you've done; that's all you will*
> *be.' It puts your mind into thinking even more in that way.*
>
> Mishka: *And it really works hard convincing other people in your life*
> *...?*
>
> Steve: *I think it did in my family. They always believed I could go on*
> *and do greater things. But at points, they'd give up and think,*
> *'He's a criminal'.*
>
> Mishka: *Or did you ever really believe it, or was it just 99%, or you*
> *thought ...*
>
> Steve: *People thought I was a criminal. I was respected because of*
> *that. As my reputation grew, I got [hesitates] ... positive support*
> *for being into crime. My reputation really pushed me into that*
> *state.*
>
> Mishka: *It's like building bars around you? Is this picture of Steve as*
> *criminal like another bar?*
>
> Steve: *I was trapped in this lifestyle and I couldn't get out and do*
> *different things.*

Issues of responsibility

These ways of working seem to provide options for exploring and challenging the foundations of imprisonment as they invite us to work with people against problems rather than punishing individuals. These ways of working do not deny responsibility for the actions that may have been carried out under the influence of crime or drugs, but invite the young men and women to take responsibility in circumstances where that is appropriate - especially in relation to crimes of violence. As mentioned previously, if you are the problem, or see yourself as the problem, then there's not much you can do about it - except maybe act against yourself. Creating space to take action against the problem, including taking responsibility for its effects on others, offers possibilities of collaboration. As Mishka Lysack describes:

> *Following the therapeutic model developed by Alan Jenkins* in Invitations to Responsibility [1990] *with men who are abusive, young people are invited to argue for a crime-free lifestyle as they assess the effects of these beliefs and practices of life in their life and the lives of others.*

Issues of responsibility are complicated and have many different threads. When working with those who are incarcerated, these conversations are occurring within institutions of degradation and the young people incarcerated are overwhelmingly from working-class backgrounds, and most are imprisoned for non-violent crimes. The problems with which people in prison present (in this case crime and drugs) have often been powerfully contributed to by poverty and abuse. The politics of gender, class, culture and age all greatly influence not only the chances of incarceration but also the construction and effects of problems such as drugs and crime. In other settings, exploring the politics of problems is often a part of empowering people to overcome the influence of these problems in their lives (see for example Grieves 1996, which describes the work of the Anti-Anorexia and Bulimia League of Vancouver, Canada). The potential for similar work in relation to issues of crime or drugs seems exciting.

A further step towards addressing the responsibilities of workers, especially within institutions of degradation where invitations for collusion in dehumanising practices are common, is the establishment of consultation/accountability processes. Later in this chapter Mishka Lysack describes the consultations he holds with those who have claimed their lives back from drugs and crime. Chapter 15 explores the possibilities of developing accountability processes to those communities most affected by the operation of prisons.

Making plans

Once young men or women have begun to separate their identity from the problem and wish to take action, the enormity and difficulty of the project is discussed and plans are made to reduce the influence of crime or drugs over their lives. Often the young men or women wish for such discussions to be recorded and distributed as testimony to their commitment:

As we explore the real effects of 'Crime' or 'Drugs' in the lives of these young people, I invite them to take a position on the problem and its place in their lives, often formalising this position in the form of a therapeutic document which is distributed to their families and friends as well as individuals in the institutions who are involved in their life, such as probation officers, lawyers, or other therapists. This document is also shared with security staff inside the Young Offenders Unit, and is placed as a 'counter document' on their case management file. These provide an alternative to the existing documents which tend to centre on problems and pathology.

One of these documents is included below. It describes the effects of crime on Stephane's life and the significant relationships in his life:

My struggle

1) *Crime keeps me away from my family. I feel disappointed with this, because I lose part of myself when I'm away from my parents and sister.*

2) *Crime keeps me from my niece xxx so that she is growing up without her knowing who her uncle is. I am frustrated with myself for being that selfish, because when she grows up I want her to know who I am.*

3) *Plus, my niece xxx is caught up in a world of lies because she asks for me, my sister and my mother say I am at school. It hurts me inside that the most important things in her life are happening to her right now, and I miss them.*

4) *At school crime keeps me at a lower level than I am able to achieve. I'm fed up with this, because I know that I can achieve more.*

5) *Crime influences me by getting me to make the wrong decisions about who my friends are. I'm not comfortable with this, because I would like to have more will-power to say no to these people.*

6) *Crime has made my girlfriend xxx very disappointed and upset with me, because right now she is making it big in the modelling world. I feel sad about this because I cannot be with her, and it's just not the same if I'm not there.*

7) *Crime keeps me going in and out of jail. It pisses me off, because I know deep down I don't want to be in here.*

Right now I'm struggling to choose the right path for what I want for my life. It's pretty obvious that I want to go straight, and not spend the rest of my life going in and out of jail. I have to decide whether I want to do crime, or be a working man.

I need support from everyone I know, including my family, staff and friends.

Date

Stephane

Witnesses and support

Once the young people have separated their identities from the problem, histories of resistance to the problems can be traced. Alternative stories to crime and drugs are explored. Examples where crime and drugs have not succeeded in dominating the young people's lives are articulated and celebrated. These celebrations often involve inviting witnesses to honour the attempts of the young men and women and to support them in their efforts.

In the Ottawa detention centre, permission has been granted for family members and peers to come into the prison in order to take part in the process. In this work the young person is invited to reflect on the areas of their lives that have resisted crime and drugs and to step fully into these new stories about themselves. Sometimes family members share with one another their own knowledges and skills in the area of dealing with powerful problems:

> *In my experience, it is often the mother who is the carrier of alternate knowledges of the adolescent, although sometimes it is other family members or even friends who know these stories of an alternative life outside the realm of influence of the problem. In the case of Steve (not his real name) and his mother, a turning point in their relationship was the realisation that the knowledges and skills which each of them could use in getting their lives back from 'Criminal lifestyle' and 'Drugs' (Steve) and 'Depression' (his mother) were the same skills which they had developed in their life together as a family.*

Rituals and celebrations to honour the changes that the young men and women are making in their lives are often held:

> *Emrys sent out an invitation to seven members of his peer group (some of whom he regarded as being part of his old life, and some of which he perceived as being part of his new crime-free lifestyle) which he read as follows:*
>
> *"This is an announcement that Emrys has graduated from his old life of drug abusing and crime, and is starting a new life with a bright future. Emrys invites you to attend a positive peer support meeting, which will be followed by a graduation party."*
>
> *The meeting focused on the positive changes in Emrys' life which had been observed by his peers. Emrys then talked about his goals, and shared a poem, which expressed his journey from his old life to his new*

one. *His friends were asked to brainstorm some ideas as to how they might support Emrys making these changes and continuing in his new direction.*

Afterward, Emrys shared his '10 favours' sheet with his friends, which he had written himself.

10 favours you can do for Emrys

1. *Try to accept the new person I'm hoping to become. Get to know the real me; I can be just as much fun even if I don't do the crime and drugs.*
2. *Don't brag to me about crime or using drugs when I'm there.*
3. *Don't invite me to do a score or use drugs.*
4. *Don't stash or even ask to stash stolen goods or drugs at my place.*
5. *Don't tempt me to stay out past my curfew.*
6. *Don't ask me to skip school or not go to work.*
7. *If you're in a stolen car, don't stop if you see me; don't even honk.*
8. *If you're planning to do a score or drugs and I'm there, let me know so I can leave and see you later.*
9. *You may not be used to me acting like a respectable, law-abiding person, but don't laugh at me or make fun of me, because that will just make it harder.*
10. *If I ever want to do any of the wrong things mentioned above, talk me out of it.*

The meeting then moved to the kitchen. We then presented a framed document of testimony, which everyone had signed as witnesses.

"This is to certify that Emrys has begun a new life which is respectful of himself, his loved ones, and the community at large. On [date] ... we, the undersigned, witnessed and celebrated his new beginning."

Emrys and everyone present either made a short speech or a toast.

Changing the culture of prison?

These ways of working also seem to offer the potential to slowly create ripples within the prison culture:

In a setting where many young people are recruited into attitudes and practices of the discourse of 'heavies' (where individuals engage in predatorial behaviours of intimidation, threats and the use of physical force to terrorise other residents), developing ways in which a young person can step away from the 'heavy' subculture into a more positive lifestyle is a priority.

Approaches that externalise the construction of 'heavy' and then gather witnesses and support can facilitate powerful turn-arounds. The following document records the 'resignation' of a young person from being a 'heavy' and asks for support from his peers:

Public Announcement - Robert

Today, I, Robert, announce in public that I have resigned from being a 'heavy'. In fact, I have been already working on my problems for a better future for some time, but now I want to make it public. I am saying goodbye to all the negative attitudes and all the things that heavies do (such as using or getting drugs, boasting about crime and drugs, and so on). I am leaving behind all the so-called rights and privileges of being a heavy for a better and new beginning of a positive life.

I am saying hello to being a normal teenager, to being a peer who is equal to other teenagers. I have been working on bringing out my strengths and abilities, which drugs, crime and negative friends convinced me to hide.

I have started my new life already. I invite all my family and my friends and others to support and help me in my life free from the grip of drugs and crime.

I look forward to putting something back into the world, instead of taking, and to contributing to other people's lives by my example, and by being a role model for my peers, from whom I am asking for support.

_____   _____

Robert   *Witness*

It is the structure and culture of prison life and the constructions of masculinity within prisons that encourage hierarchies between prisoners. Finding ways for this work to contribute to cultural change within such institutions is exciting to contemplate. Perhaps similar rituals of the public resignation of heavies could occur throughout the staff population. Whatever the case, Robert's example inspires the imagination.

Consultation

The work described above unearths and then builds upon the hidden knowledges of those who are attempting to free their lives from the tyranny of drugs and crime. Consultation/accountability practices have played an important part.

As my practice of therapy in the Young Offender Unit has developed, it has come to include a consultation group which consists of four to six individuals: 'retired young offenders', parents of 'retired young offenders', and one or two young people with whom I am currently working.

The members of this group act as consultants, commenting on articles or presentations as well as providing me with feedback and advice with regard to recent directions and developments in my work. On those occasions where I have faced a crossroads or dilemma in the work, they have been helpful in exploring the possible effects of each pathway, drawing on their own knowledges and skills and upon their experiences of working in a therapeutic relationship to reclaim their lives back from their problems.

On one occasion, I was uncertain as to whether I should continue to explore forms of group therapy in the Young Offender Unit, or whether it would be preferable to expand my practice of family/peer therapy. I presented this dilemma to the group. The young people in the group shared their experience of both forms of counselling, describing how they found meetings with their families and friends to be more empowering and helpful in constructing long-term and more durable changes in their lives. Expressing their strong preference for family/peer counselling, they advised me to de-emphasise group work in favour of working with their families and friends, a direction which I have pursued ever since.

A more recent project of the consultation group has been to start an archive or library of knowledges which the parents and teens have developed en route in their struggles to get their lives back from 'Crime' or 'Drugs'. These knowledges are documented on videotape, and are made available to other young people or parents. Another agency has expressed interest in utilising these resources with younger adolescents in a residential setting.

As consultants, these 'retired young offenders' and parents of 'retired young offenders' have also collaborated in presentations to community groups, and have participated in the production of a series of television programs on youth and families. And the group has begun to discuss the possibility of becoming a 'reflecting team' or group of outsider-witnesses for the adolescents and families with whom I am currently working, using the medium of videotape.

One 'retired young offender', David (not his real name) described his experience of the consultation group in a conversation with me. This dialogue, which is recorded on a videotape documenting his own journey and knowledges, always offers me hope for the future.

David: *Basically, you run through your activities in the last while, ways of looking at things, at problems and people, and I guess we give you feedback. We say 'that sounds like a good idea', and 'you know what helped me when I needed your help'. or 'what you did that stuck out for me the most ...' Any suggestions; it's all for the people upstairs* [in the prison], *anything that would help.*

Mishka: *You've talked about what it's like to be in counselling or a so-called 'client', and now we're talking about you being in this group as a consultant. What's it like to be on the other side?*

David: [smiling] *It's really cool. It's really neat. It's not time consuming or anything; it's once a month or maybe once every two months. It's neat not being inside. And because you were helping me before, I wonder who was helping you in helping me, who was your consultation group before - I'm not sure if you had one or not - who was on the other end of the chain?*

Mishka: *This is your chance to put back?*

David: *Every time you ask me to come somewhere or talk somewhere; it's my chance to put back.*

The work described by Mishka Lysack creates space for young people within a detention centre to separate themselves from identities of 'criminal' or 'drug addict' and to enable them instead to work against the influence of 'crime' and 'drugs' in their lives and the lives of others. The involvement of outsider witnesses, the use of documentation and rituals of acknowledgement with families and peers, and consultation/accountability processes, all seem to be powerful forces that work against the culture of the institution and create opportunities for the young people to create and step into new, preferred ways of being.

B. Reclaiming stories of self

Gaye Stockell and Marilyn O'Neill are narrative therapists based in Sydney, Australia. In early 1996, they were involved in a therapeutic group in the forensic section of a maximum security prison. The following short extract is taken from notes that Gaye made early on in the group.

Dave, one of the group, was quite willing to give an account of what life was like in prison. He spoke of it as being bad. He told of the fighting, the shouting and the noise. He said this environment was affecting his ideas about himself.

We asked Dave if the prison culture fitted with the way he thought of himself. He said, no, he was different. He remembered his appreciation of a world of peace, art, books and music. Even as we spoke the background music got louder and louder, intrusive to our conversation. There was a great deal of key rattling, door banging and outside noise.

At one point one of the other group participants leapt from his seat, stormed out of the room and was heard contributing to the increasing deafening noise. Suddenly it went quiet. Through it all Dave continued telling us of the ways that the prison culture was changing the ideas he had about himself. We enquired of Dave about any discoveries he might have made about ways he could take a stand against these threats to his identity. He told us that he could hold on to the 'cultured culture' that he knew and loved. He told us that this was a private side that no one else in prison knew about. He said he needed to keep it alive for himself.

After hearing Dave's story, another man joined in to tell us of his struggles to maintain himself the way that he and others knew ...

Alternative stories

The following interview took place with Gaye and Marilyn in May 1996 in their consulting rooms in North Sydney, Australia.

Marilyn: *There were a number of personal fears that we had to acknowledge in planning to work in the prison. We asked ourselves questions about what we might be able to offer people in prison, about the expectations for this work, and about the ways in which hope and respectful talk could be undermined in a prison context.*

We also considered what sorts of questions and processes we might have to include or exclude in order to nourish hope and a respectful culture within the group. We thought about the privileges of our position, our gender and freedom of lifestyle. We wondered about what understandings others might have about our involvement in such work, and we reviewed our own ideas about prison and how these ideas might influence us.

When we actually met with the men and started to talk it was really just a matter of wanting to hear what it was like for them. Our questions and considerations were based on genuinely wanting to hear about their experiences and ideas. We believed that the view these men had of themselves as prisoners, the view that had been encouraged by the prison cultures, did not tell the whole story about who they were. They quickly helped us to understand the ways in which the prison context had robbed them of valuable ideas about themselves. This encouraged us to continue contributing to the conversations with simple questions that made it possible for these guys to start talking about those other ways of knowing themselves. By the end of the first session, one person had spoken. By the end of the second session, I think three people had started to discover other stories about themselves.

Gaye: *We were very privileged to hear about their personal thoughts, their sort of 'separate selves', and about how they were having to really hang on to them. It was very moving, not just for us but for the other men.*

Marilyn: *They told us that was the case - that the accounts of themselves that didn't fit with the prison culture became more available and more alive as they spoke about them. Over the six weeks it was clearly more possible to talk about these new accounts each time we met.*

Early in the group we asked a practical question. We wanted to consult the men about the use of our time together. We asked if they would like a break within the one-and-a-half hours that we shared. There was no reply. We realised that this question just couldn't be answered. At first we didn't know why. We had a number of preconceived ideas about what might stop us having a conversation in a prison, such as fear, trust or even gender. But we pushed these ideas aside and we learnt that what got in the way of a reply was the fact that they were never consulted about anything in prison. They were never asked. Even asking 'Do you want a break?' was a totally foreign question. I think that gave us a real taste of the effects the prison context could have on people being able to speak for themselves, to hear their own voices, and to make discoveries about themselves.

Gaye: *Yet, at the same time, there was the extraordinary exception of Pete, who had his own voice in his head that was operating at odds with the culture of the prison. Despite the demoralising potential of the system, despite the lack of opportunities to give his story a hearing, Pete had developed a method of following the routine the prison had set him, and using the experience to gain knowledge about his abilities that could work in the world when he left prison. All of us in the group agreed that hearing about the stand that Pete was taking to predict a useful future for himself was surprising.*

Marilyn: *If there was an over-riding dominant story in the group, it was one of loss of identity. And if there were over-riding counter-stories emerging they were ones that told of reclaiming other, useful and neglected information and stories about themselves that these men felt could provide them with possibilities for more hopeful futures.*

Asking about the effects of prison culture

Gaye: *Particular questions were useful in the conversations with the men. When people spoke of their experiences of prison we would seek their understanding and often ask 'effects' questions. These included questions about the effect of the prison culture on them. They were just so amazed to be asked such questions as:*
- *What's it like for you?*
- *How does that have you knowing yourself?*

> • *How does it have you relating to your mates?*
> • *How does it have you relating to the outside world?*
>
> *They would answer saying 'Well it robs me, it doesn't allow me to know myself as a person who could exist out there, beyond these walls ...'*
>
> *One of the interesting things in my experience of groups is that you can often ask the same question of different people. In a way it's part of being visible about what you are on about. There is nothing magical or mystical about it.*

Marilyn: *And people get more ready with the answers! In working in restraining contexts like psychiatry and the prison, I have often found it useful to ask 'effects' questions that are related to the everyday. For instance:*
> • *In the course of an ordinary day, what effect would it have?*
> • *Just around here, what effect does it have?*
> • *In your relationships here, what effect ...?*
>
> *They are simple questions that invite people to speculate on what it is that is really happening.*

Gaye: *The question of how they had come to know themselves in that context was a prominent focus in those groups. It was very much the flavour of many of the conversations. These men, much more than in my experience of other groups, became very keen to explore the effect of the context on them.*

Opening space for other stories

Marilyn: *During such explorations there was another useful question. When one man spoke of becoming accustomed to accepting a lifestyle of aggression, whilst living in jail, we asked him if that lifestyle was something that fitted for him. The question 'Is that something that fits for you?' really seemed to initiate a conversation that explored his opinion of the pros and cons of a lifestyle of aggression. Questions like that invited another knowing of themselves and others in the group and freed up a knowledge of 'alternative stories' early in the conversation.*

Gaye: *We would ask questions like:*
> • *Are those ways that you are describing yourself now the same ways you would have used to describe yourself back when ...?*

> *This would open up space to reclaim, to recall other aspects of themselves. The men enjoyed questions that extended the reclaiming, and involved others, such as:*
> - *Who in the past would have known these things about you that are unrecognised in the prison context?*

Marilyn: *Or:*
> - *What would they have known about you that was different?*

Gaye: *We would explore the past for ideas that enriched their present knowledge of themselves.*

Marilyn: *We would ask:*
> - *Who would have predicted you could keep these ideas alive, especially in a place like this, where it is so easy to be robbed of them?*

Gaye: *And our conversation would fill out that story of Uncle Joe or whoever it was that could provide a different account of the man to that being constructed through the experiences of the prison culture. Like:*
> - *What else did he know?*
>
> *We would want to hear the content of the story, not just the ways of knowing. We could then come to appreciate the richness of what they were telling us and ask them what meaning this story had for them.*

Witnesses to each other's stories

Marilyn: *They told us that it was not only useful to discover new ways of knowing themselves, but having their stories witnessed by other inmates, and also hearing the stories of others, was incredibly important to them. They would say things like: 'I didn't know any of these other guys also struggled with this loss of identity'. They would express surprise about the discoveries that they made in conversations. They were quite clear that as the weeks went by it just became more natural to speak in ways that really acknowledged their preferred identities.*

Gaye: *People can exist alongside each other in the rehab in the prison, and they'll know each other for years, but they don't know each other's struggles, strengths and discoveries. They don't know the stories of each other's abilities. It seems that respect starts to develop when you have access to these other aspects of another person. The men in the group felt very privileged to be hearing other peoples' struggles and gains and victories ... So it altered the relationship they had with each other and with themselves. That's what they told us.*

Marilyn: *There was certainly a sense of camaraderie that was developed in the group. It felt as if they would leave the groups as a team. A part of the process of robbing people of their identities is through the isolation. Having a group and allowing people to share understandings in these ways has the potential to break through the isolation.*

Gaye: *It creates a sort of quiet and gentle resistance.*

Issues of violence and responsibility

Marilyn: *Issues of responsibility hovered around the edges of the groups. We had anticipated that these issues would arise. Most of the men had been involved in major violence, often involving death. People spoke of their own violence and the part that they played in that. Whether they attributed their violence to 'fear' or 'psychosis', there were still for us questions of responsibility. On one occasion when I did think that it was going to be a big issue in the group, by simply hanging in with the conversation and seeking further understanding, the person moved beyond a justification of what had happened, the deaths he had been involved with, to talking about the legacy that he was dealing with. In his case it was of extraordinary remorse because he had killed his closest relatives. He started to contend with issues of responsibility without us having to play a very directive part. However, it was something we had been concerned about and we thought we might ask questions that invited responsibility.*

People who have experienced profound interference from psychosis have suggested that sometimes control can be invited, and that sometimes psychosis can sweep it right away from them. We have concerns around attributing all actions that have been harmful, to the psychosis, or to being 'out of control', or to 'something else', because where does that leave people with psychoses when it pushes them around again? What we found was most useful in the conversations was asking simple questions like:

- *Would you tell us a little bit more about that? or,*
- *What effect has that thinking had on your life on an everyday basis?*

    These sorts of questions had people addressing issues of responsibility for themselves. They were already asking themselves those more direct questions of responsibility - we didn't need to be asking them.

Gaye: *I was encouraged by how much thinking they had done around issues of responsibility. One guy thought that if he could have someone whom he trusted and who knew about his struggles against psychosis with him, this would be one way in which he could take more control over the situation. They'd done a lot of thinking around responsibility and the illness and the part that drugs had played as well.*

Questions of accountability

Marilyn: *Throughout the groups we thought it was important to get the men's permission to ask them questions. We asked regularly what it was like to have these conversations and whether it was okay for us to continue. We explained the process we were using and what our questions represented for us. We felt it was important to acknowledge the privileged position that we were in, in hearing their stories (especially as we'd been invited by others to be there), in being able to walk out at the end of the day, and in having so many ways of knowing ourselves. We were keen for them to know that our questions came from a genuine desire to appreciate their experience, that we believed we could only develop an appreciation of this through hearing their views. They responded very generously. Toward the end of all the sessions we asked questions as to the usefulness of our involvement and the whole process:*

- *How has it been being involved?*
- *What was it like to speak of these things?*
- *What might have been significant?*

- *What might have been neglected?*
- *Is there anything that in the future we should include or exclude in our talk?*

We were particularly cautious because we had been warned, by one of the workers who participated in the group, that the things that these men spoke of, like an appreciation of art and literature, were really not acceptable within prison culture. She thought speaking publicly in these ways may have negative repercussions beyond the group. We wanted the men to be free to speak in alternative ways but we did not want to contribute to an unsafe context for them. When we checked with the men they encouraged us to continue. They continued to say right the way through that the process was useful. They said that, 'It is really allowing me to remember, to get in touch with and to interpret myself in another way'. They became more and more clear in articulating the issue of identity, of how they knew themselves in the prison culture and how they could know themselves otherwise and in other contexts.

Taking the stories forward - outsider witnesses

Marilyn: *It was very important for me to take their ideas out and beyond. Such stories need to be told and witnessed. One guy spoke of going on day leave and how he found it impossible to walk the length of Darling Harbour. In prison he never walks more than about 50 metres, so walking in a straight line was almost impossible for him, even with two warders helping. If you can't even walk in a straight line how do you survive the world?*

Gaye: *During the groups the men had wondered what effect it would have if members of the Mental Health Tribunal (who in some cases make decisions regarding their imprisonment), were to witness their conversations. They spoke of imagining if the Tribunal were above looking on ... 'how differently they'd see it, how differently they'd hear and know about us, if they were able to hear these conversations that we are having'. They felt that the tribunal members would get to understand them a lot better and that would be helpful.*

Their comments coincided with an opportunity for

Marilyn and me to meet officially with a group of magistrates. This had been arranged through the Schizophrenia Fellowship. In the last session we asked the group what ideas they would most like us to convey to the magistrates. It allowed an opportunity for them all to really pull everything together - to say 'These are the things that we would like them to know'. They were really thrilled. One of them in particular was really touched that the Schizophrenia Fellowship, that people out there, were actually thinking about what they might be thinking, and would want to present their ideas, their voice to the outside world. That was a complete surprise - that anybody beyond those walls would consider that they would have a voice or that their voice needed to be presented.

That was typical of the whole experience. That's what they reported on at the end, that the fact that we were actually interested in hearing their views, their ideas - to most of them, this was quite astonishing. So we've got a list of their ideas which we will present in order to give justice to their voices, their views on mental illness and crime.

Learning from and with those in prison

Marilyn: *There were two nursing staff participants in the group. They had requested our involvement. They wanted to develop more useful ways of working in the prison system. One was moved elsewhere before the groups were completed and we missed the opportunity to discuss with her any ideas that she may have developed about offering rehabilitation in the prison system. This was an area to which this staff person was clearly dedicated and committed. The other staff person, who worked usually in the main prison, excited us on completion of the group. As we bade our farewells, she went over to some of the men and said: 'I realise from listening to you that you have some very useful ideas and that we don't always operate in the most helpful ways. Could I consult you again about ideas that you have that might allow us* [the nursing team] *to do our job better?'*

C. Building community within the yards

The rest of this chapter explores work that I was involved with during my time within the reception and induction centre of a New South Wales maximum security men's prison. It was work that aimed to build community support within the prison yards. In 1995, two prisoners with whom I had worked previously, John Teele and Steve Morgan[1], decided that they wanted to initiate a number of groups. They stated that they wanted a space to talk about things 'other than jail bullshit' and a space in which to feel less alone. They wanted to create a place, 'to see the person, not the crim', a place to 'claim back our emotions and not let the jail take them away'. They wished 'to see the good in people' and 'to focus on the good things, not like how most professionals and groups focus on the negatives'.

As part of my job within the prison I facilitated these groups. Within them my role as an 'outsider' was to ask questions, as did other group members, and to share my life experiences, as did other group members. Obviously sometimes the questions that I asked and the things I shared were from different perspectives than those of others. Sometimes an outsider can honour stories of resistance to injustice or notice contradictions in ways that those inside a total institution cannot.

Sometimes these groups would have a consistent membership for a number of weeks, but once the original group members were sent to other prisons, similar groups were held for people who did not know each other and had only arrived in the prison a few days or weeks before. The groups did not occur over long periods of time. They are written up here in the hope that the ideas could perhaps be built upon, rather than as an example of, particularly successful work. The process described is more a gathering together of what evolved throughout different groups rather than a consistent approach.

Building community

Attempts to build community within a maximum security men's prison face a number of restraints. Prisons are institutions designed to isolate. As was described in earlier chapters, the lack of control, fear of violence, and prisoner hierarchies all lead to considerable isolation. At the same time there is often a fear on the part of prison authorities that attempts to build support between prisoners can pose a risk to the security of the institution. Despite this, the men with whom I was working were determined, and the groups began.

Introductions

After initial introductions I invited people to speak to each other about some of the things that they enjoy doing outside prison walls. For men and women prisoners in New South Wales their entire identity revolves around 'being in green', as prison issue clothing is green. This topic was focused upon in order to try to create space for each person to get another view of the people with whom they were inhabiting the yard. (I too would share aspects of my life outside my job, but obviously this had very different meanings as I left the prison after each working day.)

In order to build some sort of group solidarity, initial questions would focus on something that all members of the group would have in common - relationships with family and friends was often a good issue. Together we would explore what it takes for those in prison to maintain hope about connections with their loved ones while inside. Attributes which were often mentioned included humility, the will to go on, strength, acceptance, faith, holding on to hope, and the 'just got to do it' attitude.

Having gathered this list, I would invite the group to trace some of the restraints that prevent people from supporting each other in the yard. Together we would compile a detailed picture of the restraints. It would often include: violence, the lack of control they had over their lives, anger at the injustices they faced daily, lack of basic amenities, and the existence of 'plastic gangsters' (standover men) in the yard. Some of the more subtle obstacles that were mentioned included:

You get close to people and then they leave.
You feel really helpless when you do feel for others and you can't help them.
Confidentiality doesn't really exist in prison.
Prison culture makes it hard to trust or to mention anything that can be used against you later.

Having listed these obstacles, questions would be asked that explored exceptions, times when these restraints had been overcome. A common example was that members of the group were supportive of each other within the current or previous group session. Great acts of compassion and understanding were often expressed and witnessed.

Questions would be asked as to how such acts were possible: 'Despite the prison culture, how could these men still manage to support each other in these ways?' I would ask questions about what these examples meant. I would ask what it reflected about people's strengths, skills and knowledges, both individually and as a group, that these alternative ways of relating could be created in the most hostile of environments, even if only for short periods of time.

It became clear that the smallest of actions can have profound meanings and effects when the landscape of prison life is so barren, as Tony, a new arrival to the prison, described:

> *When I came to jail all I had was a toothbrush. I really needed a pen and paper to write with. I was really shy and didn't know who to ask. This guy here handed me one. After I had finished I went to give it back to him and he said, 'You asked for a pen, you got one, keep it mate'. It meant a lot to me, at that point in time. The little things mean a lot.*

One day the 'protection' prisoners acquired a guitar. Those in 'protection' are often viewed as informers and described themselves to me as men who were 'shunned by those who are shunned by society'. But on this day they played and sang. They filled the whole prison with their voices to the extent that guys in the main section of the prison kept shouting requests for more songs and for the group to keep playing. Questions would be asked of these moments of connection, these sparks of community that seemed to stand against the prison culture. Other examples of people supporting each another in the yards included:

- *Talking to one another.*
- *Stopping people going off at an officer.*
- *Giving someone else your phone call.*
- *Going two out* (sharing your cell) *with someone that's decent.*
- *Sharing cigarettes.*
- *Keeping people's hopes up.*

Together the groups would reflect upon these exceptions and what they said about the possibilities, and about the character, of the people in the yards. The skills and knowledges of those who were surviving prison and supporting each another in the process were gradually articulated. Openings were created. Of course, the restraints of prison life did not vanish, but the relationships within the groups grew stronger.

As an outsider to the prison culture I was conscious that even attending these groups was a risk for some. It was impossible for me to really know what was happening in the yards. Early on, when I was co-facilitating the groups with men who had spent a lot of time in prison, this was easier. I could rely on them to let me know how people were between groups and the effects that the groups were having. In some groups I could not assume that people were free to talk, nor could I guarantee that between groups people would be able to see me or relate to me what was happening. I was at times working in the dark and it felt risky. Then again, people always chose whether or not to attend.

What I heard time and again within prison was that the most important thing was to stick at a program - having someone get a group up-and-running for a short time and then leave before it finished was a common experience for those in prison, and it was almost worse than doing nothing. Looking back I have mixed feelings about this. I was unable to find ways of sustaining myself while working within prisons. At times I still feel as though I have let down those with whom I built trusting relations and friendships. Alternatively it is those relationships that sustain me now - while working on the outside.

Keeping the door ajar

One conversation within the groups has remained with me more than any other. During a discussion with prisoners who had done a lot of time, about how they managed to cope with prison life, everyone agreed that the most common ways were to shut down or to use anger and hate to spur you on. It was a conversation that spoke to me of the real costs of prisons. Never before had I heard people speak so graphically about the outrage that prisoners cannot express.

As the group continued to explore the ways in which they coped with prison life, the conversation turned to the existence of the group and their relationships. They spoke of these indicating other ways of coping. They called this other way 'keeping the door ajar'. They didn't want to close down completely. They wanted to 'keep the door ajar' so that upon release, or even during imprisonment, loving relationships of shared vulnerability might have a greater chance of occurring. In small ways they built friendships and loyalty with one another. They had not named this before, and I found it a profoundly moving analogy.

Offering something back to their communities

For many of those I was working with in prison, 'keeping the door ajar' was not enough. They wanted to offer something back. A number of men in the prison in which I worked were very clear about this and how they wished to work with young men in their communities. They asked for a welfare course to be run. Within the sociological subject we discussed the power relations involved in prisons, issues of class, culture, sexuality, age, and finally issues of gender. In acknowledgement that professionals such as myself replicate dominant power relations, I participated as a member of the group.

We tried to create what bell hooks describes as access to *forms of education for critical consciousness, that are essential to the decolonisation process* (1994, p.5). We tried to link daily prison struggles to a broader politics - politics of gender, race and class. When possible we tried to produce something tangible from the groups: a recorded song, a video to send to schools, a book honouring the stories of survival, or transcribed interviews to educate others. These become resources for further groups, further change.

Through each issue - class, culture, sexuality, age, and gender - we hoped to explore our very different positions in this culture, how we may have experienced domination, how we may have resisted this, how we may have replicated domination, and then, importantly, how we have resisted, and could continue to resist, our own forms of domination. Rarely did we have time to follow each issue through, but we began to walk what was to me an exciting path. We began the process of naming the injustices present in the room, and this then gave us scope to consider our own forms of domination.

Our final discussion on issues of gender and sexual assault will forever remain with me. As a man it filled me with much hope. Halfway through, in response to comments regarding the rights of men to expect sexual release when aroused, I found myself offering all sorts of scenarios such as, 'If you had agreed only to have oral sex with another guy in prison but half-way through he decided he wanted to have anal sex and forced you to, would that be okay?' At around this point one of the members of the group suggested that I sit down and that he take over. He asked a very simple question, something like this: 'We saw it in terms of power in the prison, we saw it with issues of class, we saw it with issues of race, we saw it with issues of age, why don't we want to see it with women?'

There was, at least in my experience of that moment, a silence, an opening. It was simply a tiny starting-point. We had not even discussed our own involvement in dominating practices, and the course was in no way accountable to those people whom we have dominated. Discussions like the one above should surely involve accountability structures to women. Quite simply it was all we could manage at the time. We managed to begin to build relations of trust between worker and prisoner. They were based on an acknowledgement of difference but also a common desire to give back to the communities from which people had come. It created the opportunity for a meeting across vastly different experiences.

When the course finished, however, the group was split up and sent to different prisons. The meeting was in many ways a brief one, and yet has had such ripples in my life. Of course I could leave the prison each day. I was being paid to participate. I was not discussing the power relations of class and culture and then returning to my cell as a working-class or Indigenous Australian man. I can only speculate as to ripples in the lives of the other men. Most are still incarcerated within New South Wales prisons and will be for many years.

As the power relations were being named and relationships built, I couldn't help but imagine what could occur if those within prisons were given the opportunity to meaningfully reconnect with their communities.

Note

1   Pseudonyms are used here to preserve confidentiality.

15

The non-traditional approach to criminal and social justice

The problem of crime and drugs has become so pervasive and so insidious it now threatens to destroy the inner city Black and Latino community. Over the past 15 years, despite all efforts to the contrary, the problem has become progressively worse. Black people are the major victims of crime, primarily being victimised by other Black people. The only solution that law enforcement officials, politicians and the media can find is harsher and longer sentences, building more prisons and declaring 'war' on the criminal, whatever that means. None of these solutions remotely resemble the answer and none have proven successful ... The communities most affected are least consulted.

Historically, some of our greatest leaders have spent time within prisons and emerged stronger and wiser for the experience. We recognise the enormous debts that we owe to communities from which we came and to which we must return ... We firmly believe that since 25% of Black youth between the ages of 20-29 are already in prisons, we must convert these places from warehouses for the 'living dead', into universities of learning, self-identity, sense of community, commitment to social change and empowerment. While this vision is expansive, those of us who have been imprisoned for many long years realise that it is our only hope to salvage our youth and it is our last chance. All else has failed and will continue to fail using traditional approaches which do not understand the true nature of community specific problems ...

Working collectively, prisoner with community, such a goal is not only
realistic but attainable. It is our sincere expectation that we can begin
the dialogue and the preparation to commence this process. (Ellis 1995,
pp.102-5)

So writes Eddie Ellis who, alongside other African American and
Latino prisoners and ex-prisoners in New York State, have developed what they
describe as 'The Non-Traditional Approach to Criminal and Social Justice'.
Where the story of this work begins is a little hard to pinpoint. It builds upon a
long history of African American prison struggle. A history that perhaps began
on the shores of Africa behind the walls of mediaeval pens that held captives for
ships bound west into slavery (Acoli 1995, p.5). A history that includes a record
of the protests that occurred immediately after the Civil War, and at the end of
slavery, when the Black percentages of the prison population went from close
to zero to 33 percent, and overnight prisons became the new slave quarters for
many 'New Afrikans' (Acoli 1995, p.5). A history that includes the 1960s and
the new wave of prison activism that occurred as increasing numbers of Civil
Rights activists were arrested, bringing with them their philosophies into the
prisons (Acoli 1995, p.17). At these times links were made between those
behind prison walls and the struggles in the outside local communities.

In September 1971, resistance within prisons, which had built up over
the late 1960s, came to a head in Attica prison in upstate New York. Prisoners
from different cultures and backgrounds took over one block of the prison and
stood together for five days, seeking to negotiate an end to their inhumane
conditions. Other prison rebellions had been settled peacefully through face-to-
face negotiations, but, on September 13 1971, New York Governor Nelson
Rockefeller ordered the retaking of Attica prison by force. Altogether 43 people
died at Attica. New York State troopers killed 39 people: 29 prisoners and 10
guards. It remains the bloodiest day of US prison history and has had lasting
consequences. In retaking Attica the barbarity of the US prison system was
exposed for just long enough to ensure that changes occurred in New York
prisons, changes that allowed a little more space for the articulation of new
ways of seeing and knowing, and for the possibility of action.

After the Attica uprising, Eddie Ellis was transferred to Greenhaven
prison where he and others formed what they called the 'Think Tank' to
continue their work to create alternatives to the prison system. Over the years
others became involved, including George Prendes, Danny Mendoza, Elijah
Ingram and Juan Rivera. These men have all been released from prison and are
currently working back in their communities on the Non-Traditional Approach

to Criminal and Social Justice. Below they describe their work and its origins.[1]

How the work began

Juan Rivera: *The history stems right back to the Attica uprising. It was the demands from that time that allowed us to create inmate organisations. We formed the Hispanic United for Progress group and they sponsored the work that we conducted. Now New York is going backwards: access to college degrees was one of the Attica demands - now that has been abolished. They are even talking of double-bunking, which was unheard of even pre-Attica! We were lucky to be caught in between the post-Attica era and what's happening now. It was a good time, a good context to put our ideas into play.*

Addressing racism

George Prendes: *There was so much racism which meant that people were divided. We tried to create a situation where we could come together. We started to teach history. History of the different groups in prisons - the Blacks, Latinos, and the poor whites so that people started to get a sense of self-worth. We grabbed all the people and said that we needed to solve the racism issues that were happening in the yards. The individuals were all charismatics and they went out, under-cover-like and cooled out the little groups.*

Gaining credibility

Juan Rivera: *Prisons mean power and control, and power and control means security. At first we had to meet in clandestine ways, under the guise of other classes. We looked around and mostly everyone knew each other because most of us came from the same area. We also did a statistical analysis and found that most people were coming from the same districts. We identified the specific locations where most of the incarcerated come from and discovered that close to 80% of prisoners in New York state come from seven inner-city neighbourhoods in New York city - the seven major communities of colour (Harlem, South Bronx, Lower East Side, Bedford Stuyvesant, Brownsville, East New York and South Jamaica). We realised that we needed community-specific approaches, not general applications.*

Seeing as most people come from these neighbourhoods then something has to happen that speaks to these communities. We reached out to the elected officials of the various communities that were being most affected by crime and prison. We made the links, targeted politicians and got them to listen to us and what our concepts were about. We set up seminars from within the prison to reach out to members of the communities so that they could hear our ideas, goals, and how we wished to go about it. Then the people from the communities put pressure on the prison hierarchy. We also had scientific data about where those in prison came from. Such pressure from outside allowed us the freedom to continue our work.

The direct relationship

Articulating this *direct relationship* between prisons and specific communities of colour and poverty was the first step in developing the Non-Traditional Approach. They then politicised the following three factors:

(i) the gross over-representation of people from these seven communities in prison,

(ii) the flow of people back and forth from these communities to prisons,

(iii) the 'crime-generative factors' that exist in these communities (such as racism, poverty, under-education, unemployment).

The Non-Traditional Approach argues that this situation justifies three major changes to the current criminal justice system: firstly, moving from the dominant individualistic notions of rehabilitation towards community and cultural rebuilding; secondly, developing meaningful forms of reconciliation between offenders and their communities; and thirdly, ensuring that all programs and aspects of the prison system are accountable to the specific communities most affected by their operation. These are the cornerstones of the Non-Traditional Approach to Social and Criminal Justice.

From rehabilitation to cultural and community building.

Juan Rivera: *The most important thing we try to teach is a sense of community. They need to understand that they belong to their communities, that their communities are their own and that they need to protect their own. Most crimes committed against Hispanics are by Hispanics. We need to protect our own neighbourhood. The powers that be don't live in our neighbourhoods. We have to stop co-operating with the powers that be by destroying our own neighbourhoods.*

  We teach a basic history of what has happened in our communities. We give a little cultural instruction. A lot of people in prison suffer from low self-esteem. It's not created in a vacuum. We teach Puerto Rican history to help them feel good about themselves. We give a historical context to what has happened to our country and then we look at the history of political struggle. We examine it, how the first Puerto Rican got elected to public office. We get people to realise that things didn't just happen. It gives people a sense of perspective, a frame of reference.

The Non-Traditional Approach describes how the viability of the notion of rehabilitation is challenged by the reality that most prisoners will be returned to the same social conditions that generated the crimes in the first place. They propose instead moving towards cultural and community-building processes.

Danny Mendoza: *When you finish the classes you become a teacher. Men start to become proud of their history. It was a beautiful experience being able to give back. It wasn't easy either. I had to go to the library, make copies of articles. I was a guy who was selling drugs on the streets. Whoever would have thought that I would be teaching people their histories! It gave meaning to my life.*

  I was so Americanised I thought that Puerto Rica was just a small island and a bunch of people on stamps. America was so big that I thought we were inferior. But I learnt about how we used to live. When I eat something now I know it came from the Taino people. I used to reject our music but I learnt of how we struggled and how the towns still have the names of the chiefs who fought. I started developing pride in who I was.

I had no history before. No basic foundation of myself. I started learning about people who were incarcerated, who did 25 years for the independence of Puerto Rica. I learnt of Albizu Campos who went to Harvard in the 1930s. I never knew this. The US offered him all sorts of jobs, but he refused to take them, he went back to fight for the independence of the island. For this he was incarcerated and died from radiation.

I learnt of Lolita Lebron who did 25 years for independence. I had role models that I'd never had. I had found a woman and a man role model and I had purpose and meaning in my life. I started to love who I was, to love being Puerto Rican. I became proud of having African blood in me, of having Indian blood in me.

As I was growing up they told me I'd have no need for Spanish, so I lost that valuable part of my culture. But then my grandparents wrote to me in Spanish - I thought it was Chinese! I had to get someone to read it for me. In prison I then started to make an effort to learn how to read and write Spanish. I traded my dictionaries - English for Spanish. I'd sit in Spanish-only groups. I began to learn how to speak. I've come a long way.

Just getting a diploma doesn't do everything. You need something that gives you a spiritual change, not necessarily religious. It's got to come from within and then we put it into action.

Reconciliation, Conciencia and Resurrection

Juan Rivera: *Dialogue needs to occur between prisoners and those communities that are contributing to the prison population. The prisoners have to be willing to reconcile with their communities, to acknowledge that we made bad decisions and want to apologise for that.*

One of the key components of the Non-Traditional Approach has been the development of a series of stages of reconciliation (African American) and Conciencia (Latino). They seek to bring together those who have committed crimes with members of their communities. They seek to do so in ways that will facilitate meaningful work and change, both on an individual level, and in terms of rebuilding community.

Danny Mendoza: *We go back to the communities and have remorse*
for our crimes and we give, we volunteer our services back into the
community. We speak of the five stages of reconciliation, or
'Conciencia' as we Latino people call it: recognition, responsibility,
reconciliation, redemption.

We attempt to reconstruct our lives by understanding first
ourselves, secondly the social environment which produced us, and
thirdly our own attitudes and behaviour towards criminal acts. In
understanding ourselves, we begin the process which reconstructs
our lives so that we become positive rather than negative forces
within our communities. At this stage reconciliation with the
community becomes possible.

We recognise that we owe the community, that we are
responsible for our actions. Those that have committed serious
crimes, have robbed or sold drugs, we claim responsibility for these
actions. Reconciliation is developing a relationship with the
community now, showing that we are for real, that we have purged
ourselves, that we have got rid of the old attitudes, old ways of
thinking. It is a healing of the relationship with the community in a
positive way. And redemption ... hopefully they forgive us. Whether
they do or not, we still have to forgive ourselves through our actions
and the community will come to believe in us.

The following extracts are taken from the Community Justice Center's
Conciencia Handout:

The reconciliation process takes place on three levels at the same time:
the individual level, community level and the combined ('linked')
individual/ community level. The method for reconciliation begins with a
sincere apology and proceeds into the Five Stage Process. This must
manifest itself in community specific action *rather than just words. The*
Five Stage Process must be seen as a joint individual-community effort
...

Recognition

Acknowledgment that we, prisoners and community elements, are
alienated from one another; we therefore need to define and examine all
the areas and levels of that alienation. The primary area of examination
is the role that the State/Establishment plays in developing our

interpretations, attitudes and actions toward one another. The Establishment provides the definitions we have of each other and triggers actions that are destructive of each other.

Responsibility

Understanding and accepting the effect of our (prisoners and community elements) alienation has had on dividing and limiting our progress as a community. This means examining the effect our personal alienation has had in maintaining division.

Reconstruction

Examines the steps required to rebuild our relationship to each other as elements of the community. This relationship must be defined and commitments and obligation articulated.

Reconciliation

Involves all of the above plus some formal statements or rite that expresses and reinforces our unification. This statement/rite must be jointly developed and represent the stage whereby the socially conscious prisoner and the community 'come home' to each other.

Redemption

The final stage takes place through our creative acts and the struggle that we engage in for our community empowerment. We redeem ourselves through the conscious work we perform together.

The Non-Traditional Approach makes clear distinctions between Latino and African American processes. However, they both share the same spirit, commitment and belief that communities, especially those most affected by imprisonment, need to create their own approaches to address issues of crime. These are approaches that will empower individuals and communities to rebuild their neighbourhoods and cultures.

Community rebuilding

Juan Rivera: *One of our goals is to grab the young people and start teaching them the basic community politics, what are the functions of people in power in our community, to try and help changes be made that are viable to them, so that young people can understand that they do have some power. Even the perception of lack of power can be a problem.*

Many of the people who have been through the Non-Traditional Approach and have been released from prison are now working with young people in their communities.

Elijah Ingram: *There is a lot of violence in schools. Kids are afraid to go to school. We have gangs, street thugs. You cannot learn if you are not safe. Kids are so disconnected from their history that the only thing that becomes important is the glamorisation of being tough. The attitude is that this is a white intoxicated school with nothing for me to learn: 'My mum's got a degree and she's still a secretary', 'There's nothing for me to learn'. The system is out of control.*

We need schools that are tailor-made, positive and motivational. An atmosphere for students to really appreciate where they have come from. A school that would help kids challenge all the major institutions rather than one that left them just not having anything to do with them. The young people have no sense that they are a part. They are categorised by their geographical location. If you are from a tough neighbourhood and you make one mistake then everyone wants you out because they are scared of what might happen next.

The first thing is to find our place. There is no hope any more. This kid says to me that his world is a big blackness. They don't care if they die. The school system is a joke to them. The teachers are so overwhelmed at controlling the classroom that it just becomes recreation and the real reason why the kids are there gets lost. The teachers are seen as jokes who smoke, party and sell drugs.

Schools and prisons are arranged from a political standpoint on the same premise. The eerie atmosphere it possesses as far as the colour of the school, the bars they hang on the windows, the classrooms are set up in similar ways. When I went and visited my old school they made me take off my clothes, go through my bag, frisk me over, put me through a metal detector. They didn't believe I'd graduated. I never got a chance to see the President or to see the teacher. It was such a similar ritual that families go through when they come to visit a prison. They are stripped of all their dignity and decency and are exposed to a lot of demoralising and debilitating kinds of encounters with administrators.

Schools and prisons are both run by bells, same classroom set-ups. They are all lined up and go out in rows just as we did in prison. They are lined up in rows of alphabetical order for eating. You have police officers in uniforms in school as well. The only difference is that they have guns on their hips in schools. They have security task forces driving around the schools all day. You can't park outside an inner-city school, you can't stand outside an inner-city school. It's the same as a prison. It is the same symbols, same atmosphere. Students are periodically stripped, frisked, all the time. I'm almost certain that teachers and staff are condoning drugs as well as being a part of it, just as in prisons. In prisons, families may bring some drugs in but they could never get in all the drugs that come in. People become addicts inside prison when they weren't outside. There are a lot of similarities.

I just spend quality time with the students, outside of the school and outside of the family. Not to talk down to them but to understand where they are coming from. Trying to find their individual gifts and individual power that can be enhanced upon. Giving them a historical background, of their own lives and of where they come from.

Community specific approaches

The rule of measure applied to all system initiatives is whether or not the focus is specifically geared to that particular community. In other words, do the system's initiatives impact in a beneficial way on the communities most affected; do the people most affected have a major voice in decision-making; are key administrators held accountable to those most affected? (Ellis 1995, pp.102-5)

The Non-Traditional Approach states that prison systems must be accountable to the communities most affected by their operation. These statements offer challenges not only to all those who work within prisons but to the very assumptions behind the criminal 'justice' system. They invite an end to top-down judgement, sentencing and bureaucratic professionalism, and turn instead towards community empowerment and grass-roots action.

Juan Rivera: *We need to start with our own community first. Ensure that it has a voice. We can't take for granted that what should be done outside of prisons is being done. We must have an active voice about things that will affect the community, it's a cycle. The people who live in communities should have a greater say in what is taking place in the system, dealing with prisons. The middle-class needs to understand that the minorities need to do this. All the decisions and all the remedies are being decided and implemented by those least affected by the problem. The people who are being affected, impacted upon by the crime rate have to be more involved. It has to be a joint effort. You have to let people in the communities validate what their experiences are. There also needs to be an understanding that the realities of the communities need to be corrected - housing, medical care, education, etc. We need to fight on both fronts.*

Note

1   The following extracts are from interviews that occurred in Harlem, New York, with George Prendes, Danny Mendoza, Elijah Ingram and Juan Rivera, in August 1995. The work of the Non-Traditional Approach to Social and Criminal Justice is written up by Juan Rivera in a book edited by Howard Davidson (1995) entitled *Schooling in a Total Institution: Critical Perspectives on Prison Education.* London: Bergin & Garvey.

16

Courting change in the USA

Clint Deveaux is an African American judge in Atlanta Georgia. In this interview, which took place in April 1996, he discusses his attempts to move the culture of his courtroom away from a place of retribution to a place of problem solving for the predominantly young African American men who come before him.

I was born in New York although my parents are from the Bahamas, where I lived until I was seven. We went back to New York and I grew up there and became very interested in African American politics and in the Civil Rights Movement. During the sixties I was in high school and college, and I didn't come south at that time. I could have - there were a number of college age kids and high school kids who came south in the civil rights days and worked and then stayed or returned north depending on what choices they made.

I came south at the end of 1969 after I had finished college. I went to law school here in 1971 and finished in 1975. For the first five years that I was here I felt sure that I was going to go back, but then I found myself running for office in the State Legislature and getting elected in 1976. After I finished in the legislature I practised law again for a few years and then went on the bench in 1981. I have been on the bench as a judge since, and haven't thought about returning to New York since probably the mid 70's. I was 34 at the time of appointment and was the youngest judge in the Atlanta community. Now I'm the second oldest on this bench - in 15 years things sort of shift!

My time here has been good but there are things about the north I miss. There are things about race relations in this town that are very disappointing and very depressing. There are things about black people's attitudes towards themselves that are very sad - they can be very self-demeaning and belittling. Sometimes they think of themselves as really not being equal and that bothers me. It seems to be a southern thing, it's not something I ever saw in New York, and that's real troubling. But there is an opportunity to help people be different. I don't know that I would have the opportunity to do this kind of work in another part of the country. I would never have been lucky enough, politically astute enough, or in a position politically to become a judge in another part of the country.

The people who come up in front of this court are adults, which starts at the age of 17. For the most part they are working or non-working poor. There are probably 25% or 30% who are middle-income or upper-income earners, but the vast majority are the working or non-working poor. At least two-thirds of them haven't finished high school. It's very rare to see college educated people. Occasionally, on a domestic violence case, you will see a college educated person, but usually in wealthy families such cases don't get to court. Often they recognise the problem and they'll send someone in the family off to a hospital.

It is very hard to see so many young African Americans - boys mainly - coming into crime and into the courts. It's pretty frightening and it's genuinely sad too. Such an awful lot of waste of really bright, intelligent, potentially decent kids who just have never had the help to focus on what makes sense, to make choices that will solve a problem rather than create a problem. They just don't have what they need to figure out how to be men in the world.

I always listen. I've gotten a reputation. They call me 'Go Slow Deveaux' because I'm always on the bench longer than other people. Quite frankly, I don't know how you can do this job without listening carefully to what people say. And sometimes it's really important for them to vent it, to just get it out. And sometimes they admit the offence without knowing they're admitting it. It helps you understand that the problem isn't that they're trying to escape the fact that they've done it, it is in fact that they don't understand what it means to have done it, and that you've got to help them understand it. They want to find other ways to accomplish their goals without violence. By and large the violence didn't work. It didn't get them what they thought they wanted. If nothing else you want them to begin to understand that, if they want something, there are ways to get it but that violence certainly isn't going to do it.

The work that I've been doing is basically a family therapy referral program. It is based on the notion that the best people to help a person figure out how to change and how to be different, are the people closest to them, the people who have known the person the longest. If a person gets arrested for shoplifting you want to find a way to understand why they are in front of you and help them understand that too. And you want to do what can be done to guarantee that they won't be back in front of you again for a similar reason. Prison doesn't really solve that problem for you, nor does giving them a high fine. Neither answers the questions that need to be answered, neither helps them to understand why, perhaps for the first time in their life, they did something so bizarre and got caught. Now maybe they've done this before and didn't get caught, in which case we need to know why the pattern of behaviour started.

I had seen remarkable success at really solving these people's problems in referrals that our court was doing in relation to domestic violence and in alcohol treatment reform. There were couples coming back here saying, 'I didn't know that we could have an argument without having a fight. I didn't know we could disagree without coming to blows. I didn't know that I could ask for something and accept no for an answer without feeling like I had to be in control.' And those were remarkable outcomes to me because it meant these people were learning.

When I first came to the bench I didn't understand that people were confused. I thought everyone could choose to do right or wrong, that you could simply choose a different path of behaviour, you could choose to be non-violent in your personal life. I just assumed that. It was how I was brought up. I don't remember my parents having a physical confrontation of any kind, I hardly remember them ever having an argument. I don't even remember them raising their voices to each other in any way.

I saw these people learning things that for them were very new and very different, so I figured that there must be something going on here that works. I began to read about how good therapy works. I then went through a divorce myself and began to realise just how angry I was at the time, and how easy it would have been to do some very stupid things

*out of that anger and out of that confusion. I realised that people often
get awfully close to the point of doing anti-social or harmful things to
others or to themselves when they are in states of confusion. I turned to
Susan Adams who helped me work out a joint custody arrangement with
my then wife around my four-year-old daughter, who's now 15. I asked
her what it was that she knew that helped her help me. She gave me a list
of reading materials and I started subscribing to* Family Therapy
Networker *and a family process magazine, and going to family therapy
annual meetings.*

*I said to Susan about a year later, 'Listen I've got a case that I
really would like your help on. Three students have been arrested and I
think that we could probably help them solve the problem'. I had finally
figured out that what brings these people in front of me is a problem. It
may not be the crime itself, but it's something that they need to
understand and get control of.*

*So we began to talk about those cases and to make some referrals.
We were trying to develop a model and to see if we could use family
therapy in a non-domestic context. We were sending people for alcohol
treatment, but to other people the system was only saying, 'Well, you did
something wrong so here's the penalty, we'll give you a criminal record,
we'll punish you, we'll make you pay a fine, maybe we'll even put you in
jail, make you make restitution'. They weren't getting out and solving
the problem. I figured that even in those cases there must be a way to
use what we knew about therapy in the alcohol treatment context and the
drug treatment context and therapy in the violence context to deal with
shop lifters and minor criminal perpetrators.*

*So that's where it came from and we developed a model that we
then expanded. The program has lapsed because I am working on
domestic and family violence now. I don't use that program in such
circumstances, and the other judges really haven't picked it up. They
probably haven't picked it up because they don't want controversy. I do
it because it's what I do. I mean, this is where I'm going to make my
mark in the world, this is where I'm either going to help people or not
help people. If I just wanted a job I'd go be a lawyer and make three or
four times as much money, but this is about trying to make a difference
in the lives of people I encounter. It's about my own religious beliefs
about connections with other human beings, and that God puts us in the
world for a purpose. There must be some good you can do with your life
while you are here, so find it and do it.*

So, even when you're confronted with craziness you keep doing what's right and try to find a way to get around the craziness or to diffuse the craziness. Earlier this year I was elected as Chief Judge of Atlanta by a 4-to-3 vote of the judges here. Months later I was defeated and kicked out by a 4-to-3 vote because I was going to bring in a Saturday Court so that people would not have to stay in jail over the weekend. One person changed their vote, switched sides, just one person. If I could have changed that one judge's mind I would still be Chief Judge and then we would be doing great things here. You would be looking at a court model of the best alternatives to prison. What was going to happen was that when the prisoners arrived at the jail, the county prosecutor and our city prosecutor were going to have lawyers who would screen the cases for the possibility of treatment. All that would happen in the courtroom, if the prosecutors agreed, would have been preparation and a contract signing to get them into the program, to set the limits and the guidelines, and to give them a reporting date and to set up a mechanism for monitoring what they do.

The next day after they kicked me out they cancelled the request. The mayor had agreed to put an extra 1.8 million dollars into our budget, but they cancelled the request for it. And the mayor then wrote a note in the budget. Every city in America is cutting back in every area. The federal government is, the states are, and all the cities are. And yet they would have put 1.8 million extra dollars into our alternative programs. We were going to have a new child-sensitive courtroom for cases involving children as victims, we were going to have a new child waitingroom. They cancelled that. All that was part of the package. We would have had a new drug court and a Saturday court and they cancelled it. So now we are not going to have any. So I just keep doing what I'm doing in my courtroom and eventually I'll convince them to do the right thing, it may take another three or four years, but it will get there.

So that's where the programme started, and I don't get frustrated. It isn't worth it to get frustrated. You just keep doing the work - and that work has been really extraordinary. In the five year period in which we were testing the model, we had about 250 defendants come through it, and it was 88, I think, who completed it to the point where the cases could be dismissed, who succeeded in the programme completely. We only had four people who were ever arrested again out of the 88, which is pretty damn good. What happened eventually was very sad.

I do get teary on the bench sometimes. I try not to - when it happens I try to say, "Listen, I've got to run to the bathroom, excuse me.' 'Usually I can recover but there are days when it is just too much. I had a guy in today whose wife was in last week while I was out, who had been accused of starving a one-year-old child. These two folk - one was 29 one was 30 - have four or five children, and the youngest was a year old. This child eventually died and the death certificate described it as malnutrition, so the baby starved to death. And neither of them appeared to be outlandishly crazy. Depressed yes, but that depression may also be a result of being in jail. Once there, without your job and then your family, you can't escape any more. All of a sudden you have to face it. I meant to remind the Corrections people to put him on a suicide watch, because when the reality hits him it's going to be pretty overwhelming. I mean, terrible as this is, you don't want them killing themselves. You know these are two thoroughly confused people.

Now, once I get to figure out what it is that drove them to the point where they could let this happen to the child I may end up feeling that there may be nothing we can do. There just may not be any way to trust these people with a child again, and you don't want them in a context where they may potentially harm someone. When I saw him come in front of me there was a look of such hollowness, I just can't describe it for you. When I first looked at him I hadn't looked at what he was charged with, and then I looked down and saw it said murder, and I looked and it said a 14 month-old child, and I looked and it said malnutrition and physical abuse, and then I understood why what I saw before me was so devoid of any kind of emotion. He just looked completely drained, thoroughly depressed. So that case has been reset for the lawyers to get ready for in a month. In the meantime, both he and his wife will be in jail and the children will be with another family.

There are days like that when I look at these people and I can't imagine a way to help them. I just can't imagine a way to do it. If I send someone for treatment, I can often visualise, once I get a treatment plan back from a therapist, what it is that's going to work and how they are going to solve that problem. I can imagine what it is they are going to learn about themselves and how much power they are going to have now to control their own lives. I can see it. I can't with these people. When you kill a child there's something that you've lost that I'm not sure you can get back. And even if you could I'm not sure that anyone else would ever trust you, especially if it's your own child.

These stories are community tragedies. There's very little thinking about the black community collectively dealing with crimes that are committed between its own members. Occasionally you'll hear a philosophical approach that will suggest that the community ought to develop those kind of ideas, but it's very rare. I haven't heard anyone speak in those terms probably in 10 or 12 years. Part of it is that we are not indigenous to Georgia. The Native American population of the United States does talk about these issues, and so do the separate tribal courts where a lot of their own problems and crimes within their communities are handled.. But there isn't an identification generally within the black community with that kind of communitarian approach. People don't see themselves as a distinct community - they see themselves as American, maybe treated differently, maybe treated worse, maybe not given all that they are due, but clearly American. They don't see themselves as separate, so it's very rare for people to talk about community focused responses.

I see that we need to raise some issues about the idea of community responsibility. I think that we could do a much better job if the black community would say to itself that we are going to take responsibility for some of these issues rather than expecting someone out there to do it. Why don't we become the community responsible for this? We've done it on some things, we just haven't done it nearly enough, and crime is definitely not one of them. Right now there are huge numbers of young African American kids involved in the drug trade, huge numbers of young African American kids not going to school and not really being cared for. All of those things are issues that African Americans ought to be dealing with, that Black Americans ought to be facing as a community. It probably wouldn't go as far as separate tribal courts and a sense of ethnic responsibility for their own, but we could do some of it. We're not even close to those. That's partly what America has done, it has made it very, very difficult for people to connect over the long term. The atmosphere is very difficult, and if you try and get people to reconcile, to co-operate in their personal lives, it's hard when the examples in the national ethos are all about being divided, conquering and being conquered.

I'm not sure how I came to all this ultimately. I know that some of it is my own experience, some of it is that I really believe that there were times in the late '50s and early '60s when this country was going in the right direction. I think that those are the things that I still hold dear and

I refuse to abandon them because times have changed. I can't imagine that I will ever become comfortable with what I see of homelessness on the streets of America. It's the desperation, it's the vacant stares in the eyes of people who have just been broken because they can't connect into the system at all. It's also that nobody cares about them any more. It frightens me to see people who feel that nobody cares about them. I don't know why I hold on to those beliefs, but I just do, despite how crazy the country is, I think you have to, you have to. I have to anyway.

Doing this work is enormously good for me. I mean, I acknowledge that I get a lot more out of this than anyone. When I say that, some of these other judges look at me and say, 'You mean you get paid well?' And I say, 'Well, I don't get paid all that well, it's nice to have money to pay the mortgage, but the real issue for me is that I learn from every piece of this stuff. I've learned how to understand the long term consequences of what happens with me and my daughter for example.'

A man I know, who's 35 or 36, has three children, the oldest of whom is a 12 year-old daughter. He comes from what we call in the United States 'the old school' - he believes in punishing with a belt, he'll whip his child. And I said, 'You know it doesn't work. You really don't want to do that.' I've been talking to him about this for years so I knew that he had backed off a little bit, and one day he said he had gotten so frustrated, upset and angry with her about something that he was about to spank her when he looked at her and realised how grown-up she had become. And he realised all of a sudden: 'What happens when she's dating a boy and the boy hits her?' He stopped and said to her, 'You know we're going to talk about this, I'm never going to spank you again. As far as I'm concerned I'm never going to hit you again. When I'm angry or when you do something wrong, we're going to figure out another way.' And it's been different ever since.

And that's what I get from all this. These people stay with me through the good things I've learned and through the things I've learned from the negative things that happen. I see the learnings played out in the lives of people close to me. It gives me hope.

For example, I hired a bailiff a year ago to work for me who had been a high school principal. He's only 54 but he had been in the school system for 30 years and he took an early retirement. He's got college-age children, a wonderful wife, and is a really nice man. He testified in court on a number of occasions for kids in this court who were 17 year-olds, juniors or seniors in high school. Other times he'd be involved with parents who had created a disturbance, or with older kids. Over 15 years I'd gotten to know him and now he works for me. The reason I hired him is because it is so clear that he's got the ears to hear that only teachers and principals have. When I saw him in front of me, in all those years, every single time I could count on him to give me a caring description of either what was going on, or what needed to be done to help that kid, or that parent, or that person who had created the problem in school. And when I had the opportunity to hire him, to have as a bailiff someone whom I could talk to about these issues, someone who could help the younger lawyers that I have in the court understand these things, I did it. Things like that make a wonderful difference.

So you know I look for all the things I have learned. I don't look to leave things behind. You use the things you learn from people and the emotions that you feel to make better sense out of your own life and hopefully to make better sense out of the lives of other people close to you. So, despite the days of frustration and anger, and sadness, and sometimes depression that comes from listening to this kind of stuff, I gain a lot more than I give out in this job. There is no question about that!

17

Circle Justice

Harold Gatensky has been involved in Circle Justice in the Yukon, Northern Canada, for many years. In the following interview he describes the ways in which First Nations People have begun to reclaim the power from police, judges and lawyers to address issues within their own communities, in their own ways. He describes how they are taking control of issues of crime and violence within their own communities and in partnerships with judges. Instead of resorting to conventional courtrooms and possible prison sentences, the communities themselves are convening circle-sentencing processes. The following piece is an edited version of an interview which took place outside of Carcross, in the Yukon, in April 1996.

In North America, specifically in the north in the Yukon, we as Native people have had quite a lot to do with the justice system. At times up to 80% of people in jail have been Native. We have a very high suicide rate in the north and we have a lot of alcohol and drug problems, spousal assault problems that we have had to deal with.

In the north it's been 100 years, more or less, since the European culture and society invaded this land. Before they did we lived quite a structured lifestyle. We had laws, we had regulations, we had communities that everyone was a part of. There were consequences for laws broken, but from the stories that our elders tell us, very seldom was there any trouble, and they always had a way of dealing with it.

The way our people used to live, the community was most

important, that was the priority. Every human being had individual rights, of course, they could dress the way they wanted, live the life that they wanted to live, but equally important was that they had a place in the community, that they belonged to the community. And the community belonged to the land because our lives were completely dependent on the land and the lifestyle that we lived. We were dependent on the animals, dependent on the trees, dependent on the fish in the waters and we were all dependent on each other.

We lived this life - my ancestors told me about this, my grandmother and my elders, they told me of this life. They not only respected each individual on an equal basis, but they also respected all of life. If you didn't treat the moose good, if you didn't treat that moose with respect, pretty soon there would be no more moose. If there's no more moose there's no more people. The same thing with the fish in the water, they were honoured, they were respected, they were treated good because again if there was no fish, if the water was contaminated or polluted, there would be no more people, no more life. All of life depended on each other, but at the same time each was quite independent and had the room and space to live its own life. From the stories we were told they lived a hard life but a very happy life, there was lot of joy and happiness and the people were content. This was before the Europeans came.

In our own community they told me a story of when the Europeans first came looking for gold. They came here for greedy reasons, wanting to take something from this land; they didn't want to give to it, they wanted to take, which was a whole different concept to our people. They hadn't dealt with that kind of an attitude in human beings. They respected the people that came here and, as was our way, showed them the best hospitality that they could. They took them in, they fed them, they kept them warm, they kept them healthy, they shared everything, but the people who came kept on coming more and more, like a flood they came to this land. Our people gave to the first people who came here the best camping area: 'Here, you camp here, there's lots of wood here, easy to catch fish, good hunting, lots of caribou across the lake here, we'll let you camp here.' Then more came and they let them camp there, and very soon what happened, as I understand it, these visitors got together and they said: 'We don't think these Native people should be living around here. Let's move them out of here.' And that's exactly what happened. These visitors that came and we showed our good hospitality to, quite ignorantly I think, turned around and started telling us how to live.

Then the gold rushers came, I think to take whatever they could from the land and leave. They left nothing good, but they did bring in the police and for some reason the Native people then became criminals in the eyes of these newcomers. Identifying that problem, then they brought the church in, because the church was going to make civilised human beings out of the savages.

In our own community, in 1906, they built the mission school. Our people were honest people. The elders, they've tried to teach us that all that a human being has is their word, so you're very careful with that word. That word is very precious to you, you cherish it, you take care of it, and when you relay it, make sure it's going to be like a rock. Make sure if you say something that your word never changes. There was no doubt in people's minds that when someone shared their word that it was the truth, that it was honesty, that it was like a stone, it would never change. So when our people came across the Europeans and they said, 'We have a better way for you', they believed them. They honestly believed them because lying or misleading was not a part of their life.

So it first began when the gold rushers came. They said: 'We have a better way for you', and we believed them and we tried our best to accommodate them. Then the police came and said, 'You shouldn't be doing this, you shouldn't be doing that, we have a better way for you'. So we tried our best to accommodate them without question, believe what they said. And then the church came, and when the church said, 'We have a better way for you', our people, being of the nature that they were, believed them, and said, 'Yes, we will try.' These people planted the seed in our people without us knowing it, that there's something wrong with us. Every time that new people came here they had a better way for us than what we had lived. From our hearts we wanted to believe that if that was the case, that if they said there was a better way, then surely we should listen and follow that way that they bring to us.

What this new way was, and what we really didn't grasp, I don't think, at the time, was not really a better way of living, but to try and be better than the next person. To try and have a better education, go to church more, do it better than. Slowly we were assimilated, taken away from our true value of equality for all of life, for all human beings, for all of this creation, slowly we slipped into this lifestyle of better than, smarter than, bigger than. Over the generations what happened to our people is that we lost our self-esteem, we lost our motivation, we lost our capability to be independent and take care of ourselves, because of course everybody had something that we should be doing a better way, better food, better this, better that. We were never accepted in society, we were never accepted by the institutions no matter what we did. They could never change the colour of our skin, and for some reason no matter how hard we tried, if we went to church every time there was a church service, if we obeyed every law these Europeans brought, if we did everything that the medical service and every non-Native person that came to this land suggested that we do, we still were never accepted on an equal basis.

Over the generations this destroyed the values of our people. We had spiritual ceremonies, we had celebrations of life. When the church saw that this was interfering with their attempts to assimilate us, they made them against the law, they put our people in jail for living their own life, they put our people in jail for doing ceremonies and trying to carry on their own spiritual beliefs.

In 1906 it was made a law that every child that was of age, which I think was five or six years old, had to go to the mission school. It was the law and if they didn't then the parents would go to jail. Some of those children never went back home for ten years, never saw their parents again, some longer, some never did make it home. They just don't know what happened to them. Children at the mission school were punished for speaking their own language, they were all given exactly the same kind of clothes to wear, exactly the same haircuts, exactly the same shoes. They were told that they should be the same as everybody else. We were told to accept the saviour into our lives and if we didn't then sometimes they would beat on us to, and as they raised that stick and lowered it down on our backside or our back they would say, 'You have to love God, God loves you'. These people represented God, and even as a little kid you figure, 'Well, if this is who God is, I do not want to have nothing to do with it'. I am sure all those people who came out of the mission schools were convinced that they were going to be punished, that they were going to hell and that was it, so what was the point of even trying to do good?

They were punished for many different reasons. So many of those children that went to that mission school were sexually abused, a thing that was almost unheard of amongst our own people, and they were physically abused. Before this it was almost unheard of amongst our own people, although it did happen occasionally. Now there was a generation of children that were being shown this, shown a way of life. Many many of those children who went to the mission school were sexually abused, many of them. Many kids tried to escape, but they always caught them when they went back home. Their parents wouldn't want to go to jail so they'd send them back, as much as it hurt them.

If there was any trouble in the community it was always a Native person first - they were the first ones they would look to if there was any kind of trouble. If people even went out and hunted and fished they made it against the law. We were stuck completely, stuck into a lifestyle that was a dominant lifestyle, whoever had the biggest stick had the most power. To us it turned into a sickness, a disease. Our people felt a very empty place in the heart. They turned to alcohol and they drank in excess. They had no values to uphold as our ancestors did, and they weren't accepted in society so they spent a lot of time feeling like failures and living in apathy. A lot of the young people who were sexually abused in the mission schools turned around and did the very same thing to their children.

The RCMP [Royal Canadian Mounted Police] came - well it was North West Mounted Police first, but then RCMP. We were never accepted on an equal basis. The police had their own way of taking care of things, and the first thing was to scare, intimidate, beat the crap out of you. Then of course you'd go to court anyhow, after they'd beat the crap out of you, after they'd scared the living crap out of you. Then they'd go to court and they didn't hesitate to lie in court to convict somebody. Here we are told to swear on the bible: 'To tell the whole truth and nothing but the truth, so help you God', and we took it quite serious. But then to hear these people who are supposed to represent the law and uphold the law get up in the court and say, 'Yes, he did it, yes, I seen him do it', and he was 20 miles away, it makes you wonder what's been going on.

From 1906, it's been three or four generations in the Yukon now, our people have had no parenting skills, a lot of them, a lot of them are victims of sexual abuse, violence, a lot of them are permanently disabled from some of the beatings and abuse from RCMP. And so as it turns out now that 80% of people in jail are our people, and people still today say, 'What's the matter with them?'

Then the government came in and said, 'We are going to take care of you now, we're going to build you houses, we're going to provide *dental for you, we're going to provide your medical care, we're going to take care of all your needs'. And of course, like little children, we let ourselves become dependent on the Department of Indian Affairs, a government agency that has no heart, no compassion. They just go through a process - this is the rules and regulations, we have to take care of these people, so let's do this, let's see what it says under section B1 for dental plan, okay we go in and do it - and I mean it was quite the thing for our people.*

I went to the mission school myself, actually when they built the Alaska highway here in 1947 or whenever it was. My father came up and worked on the Alaska highway with the crew that came up here - that's how my mother and father got together. My Mum and Dad split up when I was eight years old. My Mum, with four boys, had to try and take care of herself and us at the same time, so she put us in the mission school. I went to the mission school for two years, and I remember very clearly what it was like. I was convinced I was going to hell by the time they were done with me, I knew there was no hope for me. I was convinced I was stupid by the time I was in grade 4 or 5 going to school. I was convinced I was dirty because I wasn't the same as everybody else. By the time I was a teenager I was convinced that there was no hope for me in this life, and I didn't really know what my place was here.

I suppose trying to prove that I was something got me caught up in the justice system. I got charged for assault when I was 14 years old, went to court and got probation or something. When I was 15 years old I got charged again and I was raised to adult court and sent to jail for six months in Alberta. It was a funny thing for me now, when I think about it, because I truly was convinced that I was worthless, hopeless, incorrigible. I heard that term, I didn't even know what it meant but I heard social workers saying it, using that term and I thought, 'It sounds really bad, it must be bad, don't sound good that word'. When I used to go out and drink I could try and act like I was some kind of a big shot, which I wasn't, but at least I could pretend then, it felt somewhat important in a sick way. When I used to fight with people, others would come from all around and gather around and watch, and they would cheer me on. Sometimes they would be cheering the other person on, but when they cheered me on I know I felt like: 'Wow, these people appreciate something here, I am good at something. They do recognise it', and that sort of perhaps dominated my self-esteem, my journey towards self-esteem: 'C'mon Harold, you can do it, beat the shit out of him, way to go, yeah, right on'. After a fight was done they'd say, 'You give it to him good', and I guess in a sick way it made me feel - 'cause I was sick then, only I didn't realise it - it made me feel important.

Of course then I went to jail. I was 15 years old. I was terrified. I was living with my Mum and going to school, and the next thing I know I was in jail. In the jail it's a very sick society where there's a king pin and then it goes downhill from there. You know, depending upon how intimidating and how tough you are, it depends on what place you hold in the jail. You know that people are going to be bullying you all the time, they gonna be taking things away from you all the time, they are going to be making your life miserable while you're there - well, if you were weak that's what would happen. So at 15 years old when I went to jail. When they sent me to Alberta, I did get picked on a lot, until finally one day I got sick and tired of it and I beat the living crap out of this guy who was bullying me all the time.

From then on, every time somebody gave me a little bit of trouble or something I would beat the crap out of them if I could. No more problem. They wouldn't bother me any more. I also developed a look on my face that the meaner, the more miserable that I looked, the less people would bother me in jail, and so I got to looking pretty mean and nasty as a 15-year-old kid. By the time I was out of jail I was one mean dude who didn't take no crap from nobody, who knew how to resolve his problems, beat the shit out of them if you could. Of course when I got out of jail it wasn't too long before I was back in again for assault, getting drunk and beating somebody up. I remember it very clearly, although it's well over 20 years ago. I remember the feelings, I remember the people.

I also remember that in that jail I met some very nice people, really good people that I had seen out in the street, couldn't figure it out, the nicest people but every time I had seen them out on the street they were really drunk, they were in trouble. I would just pass them right by. But when I got to know them in jail, my gosh, they were nice people. They'd be friendly, they'd give you smokes, they would sit down and talk. They had stories to tell, they had things to share. They were quite talented, quite capable, a lot of very resourceful people. That's something that I never did forget.

By the time I was 18 or 19 years old it wasn't unusual for me to wake up in the jail cell the morning after I had been out on a bender. It was a routine: go out, get drunk, get arrested thrown in the drunk-can, get up in the morning go out and then sit around with your friends and tell them all about your experience like you had made some kind of accomplishment or whatever.

One time I woke up in the jail cell in the morning and I hollered at the guard, I said, 'Alright, get me out of here', and the guard came in and said, 'You're not going any place'. I said, 'What do you mean? I'm sober, get me out of here, I'm done'. He said, 'No, you've got some charges'. I said, 'No, you've got the wrong guy, it's not me'. He said, 'You've got assault causing bodily harm'. Some guy came into the jail just then and he looked in the cell at me, some guy who I swore I had never seen before, and he looked in the cell at me and he angrily pointed his finger at me and started shaking it and said, 'That's the guy - he's the one, he's the one who did it.' I said, 'Oh no, you're wrong, I didn't do nothing'. He said, 'He's the one', and I ended up going to jail for a year.

But that morning when that man came in there and centered me out, pointed me out, I knew myself, I guess somewhere in me I knew I must have done that and I just sat down and I thought about it and I said: 'No, no, no, not for me, this is not the life I want to live. If this is all there is to life, what's the point of even being alive? If there's nothing else then this is disgusting.' So I guess I made some kind of commitment to myself then, and said, 'That's enough of that - it's not the life I want'. I did end up spending a year in jail, but when I did get out I knew I was going to try and live a different life and I never did go back to jail. Not that I didn't get in any more trouble, I just was a little more careful and I didn't get caught. I'd had some good training. You learn a lot of things in there. You learn, like I say, that mean look that I still carry today. When I get amongst a bunch of people I put my mean look on, just like a mask, if I don't want nobody to bother me. I just look very stern and mean. Sometimes people will come up to me and say, 'Whoa, scary, look at you!' and I catch myself doing it because I really don't want to be like that now, but it's something that I was trained to do.

I told myself I would never forget those people in jail. I suppose I had a spirit living inside of me, not knowing it, not acknowledging it, because I was pretty much still convinced I was going to hell. But as I got a little bit older, I started to think about that spirit and I started to wonder if there was a little bit more to life than what I had understood myself or what people had relayed to me. I could see it in the land, I could see, you know, the peace of the land and I could hear it in the wind and without knowing it in the sun, and I'd go out sometimes to a lake and it would be a beautifully calm day, the birds singing, and it just brought out a feeling in me but I couldn't really identify what it was, but I suppose it made me pursue, you know, to try to find out what it is.

I went through many different beliefs and many different churches and different concepts of what spirituality is, the Mormon church, Pentecostal church, shopping around looking for something, but I never did find it, never did. I be doggone if I didn't fall asleep as soon as the pastor started talking. I couldn't hold my head up. There was no way, my eyes kept on closing, my head started dropping and I'm sure I started to snore, and no matter what I tried to do, I couldn't stay awake. I felt so embarrassed and humiliated I left the church and I never did go back. I felt, 'No, this is not for me, not for me'.

Then, you know, later on I started to get myself kind of settled down, got married, got a job, worked for a long time, and even after I did that for a while, it still didn't feel right to me because I'd seen this society, I'd never fit into society no matter how much I may have tried to. Actually, the more I seen of it, the less I wanted to fit in to it. Everybody I worked with - once in a while they'd get a new car and they would make their payments, or they were going to buy a new house. For me, if I stayed in a tent it was fine, if I stayed in a old rundown shack that was good enough for me, as long as my car ran I didn't care. I didn't want to have a new car, I didn't want to be a slave to the bank, so I guess I was kind of an outcast or whatever you want to call it, rebel perhaps.

After I worked for one place for seven years, I got tired of it and I said, 'I'm going to go outside', and I went down to Vancouver Island, and got involved in churches and what-not again. But one time I went to these dancers, long house dancers down there, and these people, they spirit dance, and I'd never experienced anything like that. I just went and watched and it really felt good to me, there was something there. I knew that they had accepted me. You know, they welcomed me into their house, although I wasn't a participant, just an observer. I certainly felt accepted, which was something that was very rare to me, just to feel that, and that I suppose kind of turned me towards thinking about Native spirituality; and although it was quite an experience for me on Vancouver Island to see what they were doing down there and how much of their own culture and spirituality they had hung on to, even though they've gone through very similar experiences as we had in the north, it still never really helped satisfy that something inside me that was looking, searching.

So after three years on Vancouver Island I came back home and I came back to Carcross here, and my people were so happy to see me again. I really felt like an outcast when I was in trouble with the law and that, and I suppose it kept me away for many years because I was sure, without even thinking it, that my people would want to have nothing to do with me - there was no 'my people' then. Then it was just: 'There's a bad boy, there's that bad boy again, let's get out of here before he makes trouble'. So when I came back my people accepted me, my relatives were happy to see me, my friends, people I'd grown up with, and my grandmother, although she had long passed away, some of the things that she used to teach me when I was a little kid started to make a lot more sense to me, some of the stories that she'd told, some of the good things that she's shared, they took on a different meaning.

I went to a sweat lodge ceremony. I'd had many opportunities to do that but this one time, I guess, I suppose I started to believe in The Creator. I said, 'Yeah, I believe', and I thought that was enough. 'Hey', I thought, 'maybe I'm not going to hell now.' But I still felt very confused and mixed up. I'd split up with my second wife, I had three boys by her and I knew that my marriage had failed, and again it brought out those deep feelings of being a complete and utter failure in this life, and I knew I needed help. That even though I had come over my experiences to believe in the Creator, that it wasn't enough, I needed help. And so I went where I knew there was a sweat lodge which I'd heard of - it's an Indian church, Indian hospital, Native ceremony - and so I went to it, my brother and I. My brother had been going for some time himself.

The funniest thing, when I went to that ceremony, it's a ceremony where you build a lodge out of willows, it's a round building, small place, dig a pit in the middle, heat up a bunch of rocks red-hot and you bring them inside and you have a bucket of water, you pray and you pour water on, it gets very intensely hot and you pray, sometimes you just pray to make it through it, pray that you're gonna live, and boy, oh boy, was it ever not quite the same, quite different from anything I'd ever experienced. I knew when I went to that ceremony that one time, that first time, when I went to that ceremony I knew that that's what I had been looking for all my life. I had found it, and I also knew, which was rather ironic, that it was right in my own backyard the whole time. I'd spent my whole life, over 30 years, looking for something and there it was right in front of my eyes the whole time. I guess it wasn't my time to see it. My own people's way, my own people's belief, my own people's values, my saving grace, my redemption, my path for hope in my life.

All of a sudden I felt that I wasn't worthless, that I hadn't screwed up so bad. I understood that every human being on this earth screws up in their life, some just do a lot better job of hiding it than others. I realised myself then that all those guards that were dominant and always constantly picking on people at the jails and making their lives miserable were no different than the very inmates that they take care of. I realised that the judge who sits behind that big desk with the gavel in his hand somehow making people believe he's the closest thing to God was no different than any other human being on this earth, and I knew that everyone of them had no more of a chance of being accepted by The Creator than anyone else did, and I had just as much a chance as everyone else, and I learned to forgive myself. That was a big step for me.

Then I turned my thoughts and my heart towards other people, my own people, the ones that I had seen suffering so much in my life, the ones I'd seen in the mission school that were still suffering, the ones I'd seen in the institutions, the jails, the hospitals, the whole thing I seen, I wanted to help somehow. So I became a helper in the sweat lodge ceremonies. I started to be trained to be just a helper, but boy, I got a lot out of it, and I got a lot out of seeing people coming there, that were just as crippled as I was, getting help and encouragement and strength, and it was our own people's way. Again our values, our understanding, our elders, our way. Nothing else in this world helped me like that, nothing.

An opportunity came - they asked one time, they wanted something in the jail that could help the people because of this repetitiveness of people going in there, because of the bitterness that they could see building up in people the more they came and went and came and went, and the frustration of not being able to do anything with them. An opportunity came for us to go into the jail with this ceremony. Of course, for me, because of my own experience in jail and because of my experience at the ceremony I whole-heartedly agreed to go in there and do it. I could see that it did start to make a difference for people, it did help them, and I was just a helper then myself, but it was something that made a difference. The other thing I realised when I started to acknowledge my own people's ways and the values that they had, was the power of the circle. I've sat down with people in a circle and I experienced equality. I can say what I feel like saying and it will be accepted. I was listened to, I was respected, I was heard. So we went in to the jail in this circle setting. We gave people the opportunity to share some of the pain, some of the hardships that they had experienced themselves, and I knew because of nature that this was the way - the gift The Creator had given to us was the circle. The sun is in a circle, the moon is in a circle, the trees are in a circle, the birds make their nest in a circle, the beaver builds his house in a circle, you drop a rock in the water in a pond and it makes a circle.

We had been trying to put this circle into a square, stuff it in there and make the circle square, and that's where our trouble came from, and so for me it was like releasing something that had been squeezed up and misformed. The circle came back into my life. The circle of life, our lives are in a circle. I mean, it goes on and on, we could talk all day long just about the significance of the circle in life on this earth. I started to understand that if you can help put people in a circle in a safe atmosphere you never know what's going to happen, because that circle invites a greater power, greater than anyone of us. It opens up a door between this world and the spiritual world and it really is a powerful thing.

One day I started to involve my brother, and we both got quite involved in the circles in the jail. We knew most Native people in the prison because we all went to the mission schools and we've all spent time in jail together. Anyhow I started to pack knowledge in those people, their goodness, their values, and I started to try and encourage people to do good. God, if I can do good, if I can make it out of that, if I was so messed up myself, so screwed up and I made it, surely these other people could. They certainly had a lot more natural resources available to them than I did. I tried my best to encourage, and I got this one thing that my grandmother told me a long time ago stuck in my heart - it was that not until every one of us are healthy again, not until every person is fed, not until every person is warm and taken care of, then things are good, then things are going good and that's a good life. So for me, I thought, okay, I made it out of that jail, my own people's values helped me. For some reason it rang true in my heart: not until we get our people out of there, not until we've helped everyone that we can, not until we pull that last one out, then we are okay, then we've done our job and it's good, it's good for us.

So when a judge came to the community, of course we encouraged this idea of the circle. At the same time I was of kind of going through this transformation, this healing process, many other people were going through the same thing, similar lives going through that and managing to recover. It was happening right across Canada, right across the north; it was happening all over the place from what I understood. So I realise that when a judge came here one day, one judge who had a kind heart and was compassionate and caring enough to say: 'Look, I'm getting sick and tired of sending these guys to jail. It's not doing the jail any good, it's not doing them any good and it's not doing your community any good for these people to keep on coming and going like this. Is there anything different that we can try?' And somehow he had heard about the circle somewhere, and they had tried one in the north, a little bit north of us, a community sentence circle and he was quite impressed with the results of it. They tried it there with a guy who was a repetitive offender, constantly repeating offending. And so for us, when he came here, he asked me about it. I don't know how he came by asking me, because I certainly wasn't any kind of authority in the community or anything, but he did ask me, he said, 'Would you like to try this Circle sentence?' and, as soon as I heard him say 'circle', I knew myself that it was good because it comes from the Creator to me. So when he asked if you want to do circle sentence, I said, 'Yes' without any hesitation. I said, 'Yes, we do'.

All of a sudden I was the spokesperson for my people, self-appointed I guess, but I said, 'Yes'. He said to me, 'When would you like to do this?' He said, 'We'll take some time, we'll talk to these people, get this group together. What do you think? Next court appearance?' I said, 'We'll do it today'. And he looked at me kind of funny and said, 'What, today?' And I said, 'Yes, today, let's start it right now.' And so he went out and said, 'Okay, we'll give it a try'. We went out and gathered our people what we could, the ones who could appreciate the circle and recognise the power and recognise there's an opportunity to help our people who are a little less fortunate caught up in that system.

We went out and gathered them up and we all gathered in the community club and we all sat in a circle. We used a little sweetgrass sage, smudged ourselves, we opened up with a prayer, we all held each other's hands, victim, offender, Native, non-Native, judges, crown prosecutor. My god, what a feat that was! We held each other's hands in the circle, and we said a prayer, and we asked The Creator to help us:

If there's anything good can come from this, please be with us and help
us;
guide us, guide our words, guide our hearts,
help us to help those who are less fortunate,
to help the families in our communities
that have been affected by this attempt at assimilation,
by the horrors and tragedies of life that we have lived,
let us now do something good and contribute.

*Then we all sat down. The judge said, 'You know this guy's looking
at six months in jail unless we can find an alternative'. So all the people
got together and said: 'Gosh, why don't we get him fishing for the
elders, feeding the elders again? This guy's very artistic - let's get him
up in the school teaching the young kids how to carve. There's got to be
stuff we can do', and we all talked about it. There were some people said
we should throw him in jail, 'He's a good-for-nothing, no good having
him around, he's just going to do it again', you know. We answered to
that, you know, we said, 'Who are you anyway? We've never seen you in
Carcross before. You come in and tell us to put our people in jail. How
many times you been to jail?'*

*The crown prosecutor said, 'Surely this guy should go to jail?' and
he read off his criminal record, which was quite extensive, and we said,
'How can you come' - we asked the crown prosecutor in this circle,
which we had never had the opportunity to do before in our lives, 'How
can you come to our community once every second month for one day
and be such a good judgement of character of these people? Say they
are all good for nothing, lock them all up? I mean, did you live with
these people? Have you seen these people in the community? Where do
you get this information from? Is it just off a piece of paper that you
have?' And we asked the crown prosecutor, 'Are you going to be here
when he comes back to this community?' And we made him think about
it. One of the people in the circle said: 'This is a good man here, he is a
good man, we know him, and he's very well liked and respected in this
community. Yes, he's made a mistake, yes, he did, he was frustrated, he
got drunk and he did some stuff he shouldn't have done, but that doesn't
mean that's the whole person.'*

*The amazing thing about this circle sentence was that it pulled our
community together. There were people in that circle that had never
been in the courtroom unless they were charged for something and they
were there in a whole different concept. They were there to help, they*

were there to contribute, they were there to support and it was an amazing thing to have so many people in our community come together in that way, really it was incredible.

To be able to respond to the crown prosecutor: 'Who is this guy who comes to our community and says we are no good for nothing anyway? You know, sitting there acting like he's sitting on the right hand side of God or something!' He was put in his place, much to the pleasure of everyone else in the circle. But in a nice way so that it made him think perhaps, whoops, maybe I have been making a mistake here, maybe these people aren't so bad, wow, look at all these people come out to support this guy - how can he be so bad if he has this much support? The judge took our recommendations into consideration and the guy was sentenced to go out and fish for the elders, he was sentenced to do community work for the elders, he was sentenced to go to the school and teach them art, he was sentenced to make restitution for the windshield of a car he had broke and to go and apologise to that person who he had offended in that way. We were happy with that.

When you go to the elders again it is still a wonderful thing when you give them something. What it did was it started putting this guy back in the community where he had isolated himself, a feeling that we know very well, people who have been through it: 'I'm no-good-for-nothing, I can't make a contribution or nothing'. So when our sentence for him, in the circle sentence, put him back into the community, he was feeding the elders and he was teaching young people and it gave him a sense of, yeah, he did belong to this community. He did get in trouble again one more time, but com-pared to his criminal record he's doing pretty good, he's thinking about it now, he didn't know so many people supported him. Of course after his court order, his proba-tion order, all of a sudden everybody in the community had their eyes on him, it wasn't just going to jail for six months and getting his time done and then getting back on with his life, all of a sudden everybody in the community was watching what he was doing, and wondering was he a man of his word, did he understand that when he gave his word that it was important? Did he realise that his word was the only thing that he had and would he honour that? So we watched him, everybody did and it was kinda hard on him actually, kind of hard with your whole community watching you. It's our own people's way, it's our values, the very thing that European dominant society tried to take away from us since they set foot on this land, now that's what's helping us recover.

Ironically my brother and I are now back in the jail doing Native spiritual ceremonies - the very same ceremony that they put people in jail for is now in the jail to keep our people out. It's kind of come full circle. Now our people are realising it's their own values, it's their traditions, it's the knowledge of the elders. A lot of them are, not everyone. There's a lot of people who are assimilated but a lot of them realise now that it is up to us, we can no longer give it to the institution of RCMP, medical service to the church, to society to solve our problems for us, now we realise that it is up to us. Wherever it is, in this land it is for the people to come up with what they believe is a solution, surely that is going to be what works for them, surely it is. It worked for me in my own life, it's working for many, many people now in this land across North America, the recovery of our people, the recovery of the aboriginal people in North America, and it's not a law that has been passed by parliament or anything else like that, it's our own people who for some reason have been moved to be involved to say there could be a better way.

We speak to the hearts of people, we don't speak to their heads. We've had enough of that, it doesn't work, we speak to their hearts. We say, surely you can give people a chance. The big difference in a circle setting is that we have the capability to forgive, we have the capability to say, let's put it behind us and get on with our lives, we have the capability to give people a chance, to just give them a chance, and then it's up to them to do with that chance what they want. If they want to just throw it out the window or cast it away, at least we know that we tried, that we tried something that we are not all sitting and saying: 'Did you hear that so-and-so got six months? or, 'That guy, he's gone for a couple of years. Oh well, he had it coming to him.' Now we are saying we tried, and that's the biggest thing I think. We've always had that in us. All the Native values in this land, spiritual values, ceremonial values, are coming back, the power to forgive. Honesty comes from within, it's not something that you can impose on people.

Now I'm working towards helping my people, to forgive them, to give them a chance, to let them feel like, yes, they are important, they do have something very valuable to contribute, people do care for them, a community, you know a people that are caring, a family, whatever it may be. And I believe and I hope that I see it in my life time that we are going to see our people out of jail. The amount of Native people in jail in the Yukon dropped significantly when the communities in the Yukon started to do this circle sentence, when the communities became involved, when the elders became involved, when we tried an alternative to the institutional process that we had all been going through. When we tried to involve everyone. Like the offender - what is it that made him feel like that? Let him say it in front of his people. Perhaps it's something that we didn't even know, maybe somebody passed away recently in his family or maybe the sheriff just came in and confiscated every bloody thing he ever owned because he couldn't get a job because he's Native. Whatever it may be, let him talk, let us hear what he's got to say, and let's see if we can hear in a circle setting the regrets, remorse, acknowledging the mistakes that were made. That's all we need, then we'll go from there and hopefully we'll never give up, we'll keep on being involved.

In relation to the circle, the big thing that I find that really gets people in the right frame of mind is if you talk about yourself, you know, can you talk about yourself openly and unashamed. If you can say, yes, I suffered this, I've been to jail, I've had a problem with alcohol, I've recovered from it, but these are some of the things that I had to deal with. I reveal myself to people, that I'm no different, I'm no better or no worse, that I'm on an equal basis with them. And that brings out the spirit of the human being in our people too, you know it gives them: 'Oh gee, it wasn't only me. I'm not the only one who feels like that. I think I'll tell my story too'. It starts people going like that.

When we looked at our community and asked: 'What can we do with these people? What is an alternative to jail for them?', we realised we haven't really been given too many options, you know - it's either jail or probation. And when they put people on probation you know they're doomed to fail. You're on six months probation, you're on a year's probation, two years, and when you know what the conditions are on their probation you know they're gonna breach.

A lot of the people that are up in the jail right now are there for breach of probation. They were doomed to fail. You tell an alcoholic, all right, you can't drink any more, but you know they're going to set up conditions and an environment where they have no choice but to drink. They're masters at it without even knowing it. You have to be really careful with this probation stuff. People can willingly try and accommodate and instead set them up for failure, to fail again, and again and again and again. Surely to goodness, after we fail so many times, it can't help but make us feel that we are failures.

Let it be a lesson to them, instead of a punishment, and I think that's the difference between circle sentence and the regular justice system. They want punishment, but what real lesson is there in that, except to be a little bit smarter next time and don't get caught? We need to let people learn by their mistakes and let them grow. We try our best not to stop that learning process but to bring to people's awareness that there's a lesson in life that needs to be learned.

When we do look at alternatives, one of the most helpful things in my own recovery - getting on my own two feet again, of coming from, 'You no-good-for-nothing, you'll never make it', to thinking, 'I'm okay, yes, I've made mistakes, but I've learned from them, and I do have some importance in being alive on this earth', is that I went out on the land, this land here. I went out on this lake, it goes 120 miles down here.

When I went out on the land I remembered again the stories that my grandmother told me. She talked about all of this life, about four-legged, about winged, about the fish and everything, like they were people, like they were beings, the beaver beings, the coyote beings, the moose beings, the big long cloud being, the grizzly bears, like they were people, like they were neighbours. That's the way my grandmother talked. So when I went out, and I started going out more and more often on this land, I realised that I was a part of a wonderful, wonderful part of this natural land, and that all of this life around us accepted me as I was, it was not judgemental. I realised I had a place out here. I remembered the stories about survival, and I started living that myself. I had to learn to live, but man, oh man, did it ever make me feel good, by golly - I was able to take care of myself, I was capable of doing something. I did belong out here, this is my place, and my nature is out in the wilderness, out in the bush, 'cause that's the place where I had to obey the laws or really suffer the consequences. Not man's law, but the laws of nature itself.

We've come through a lot as Native people, we've survived a lot and now come a full circle. It's the very thing that society, that the European society tried to strip away from us, that is our most powerful healing tool, for any people back to nature. All of life has a spirit, the sky has a spirit, the sun does, every human being does, every tree, every blade of grass, every mosquito, everything has a spark of life in it. For us to acknowledge that once again, to recognise it, here we find it very easy to relay that message in the environment that our ancestors and our elders were raised in, and in the environment where we truly belong, were homesick for. We don't even know it ourselves, but once we find ourselves back in that place again then we feel good and we are on a healing path. For other people, too, you know, who is it that's going to relay this message, who is it that's going to be the spokesperson for nature now? Who is it that's gonna help those people who are in a vicious circle of institutionalisation from the street into jail, into the street into jail, who's it gonna be?

It's gonna be the very same people that have gone through that process themselves, they are the most powerful helpers, they are the ones that can represent and speak from their heart and accept people on an equal basis. Those are the people that need an opportunity, a chance to express themselves, they need to be heard, they need to be nurtured themselves and given an opportunity to share the message that they've gathered up through the hardships of this life. They have a message for people. Given a little responsibility, it's amazing what these people can do, and there are so many now that are coming around and making a difference, they are contributing, they are helping.

No, it's not these people that have gone through university, it's not these people who have sat in judgement of others all their lives, it's not the person with the biggest amount of zeros in their bank account, it's the people who have suffered, struggled and survived, that now have a message to deliver to their people, and their people are those that are less fortunate, those that are struggling.

Surely the healing in this land is worldwide now, the recovery of people, the healing of people, putting the spirit, putting the life back into all things around us. That's a way of life, and every person has a place in it. You have a place, everybody does, every human being has a place if they can shed that skin like a snake, shed their old ways and you know come open-hearted and open-minded to a life of equality. It's a wonderful thing. Put people in the wilderness, give them a chance, let the community give them some responsibility, listen to those people that have been through the institutional life, listen to their experience, to their story, give people a chance.

What it has done for us is given us hope, hope is the people for recovery. That was something that we never had, something that we all wanted. Now as our people become more involved, there is a beam of hope. It's a powerful thing to have hope in your hearts, really powerful. We're gonna make it, by golly, I think we're gonna make it.

18

Maori and youth justice in Aotearoa/New Zealand

The powerful story of the resurgence of First Nations People in the Yukon is in some ways echoed in Aotearoa/New Zealand. Here, perhaps more than in any other country, Indigenous traditions of justice have begun to have a profound influence on the mainstream justice system. Originally, in the adult court system there was no jurisdiction for traditional Maori justice. Since European invasion, Maori people had been denied the right to sentence their own people in traditional ways, despite the agreements of the Treaty of Waitangi which clearly state that Maori laws and customs were to be maintained (see Jackson 1990). Despite this, local Maori people have, on many occasions, prevented police action by dealing with offenders in traditional ways when the offences have been costly to other members of the Maori community. Some *marae*[1] court sessions have lasted up to three days (NZPA, in Consedine 1995, p.81).

Michael Doolan, Southern Regional Manager of the New Zealand Children and Young Persons Service, states that, in 1984, the Labour Government sought to overhaul the Juvenile Justice system for a number of reasons:

- *There was a growing dissatisfaction ... about the effectiveness of work with young offenders ... gradually a loss of confidence in the goal of rehabilitation built up.*
- *There were new and more determined efforts by Maoridom to secure*

*self-determination in a monocultural legal system that demonstrably
discriminates against Maori and places little value on Maori customs,
values and beliefs.*

- *Related to Maori concerns, but also an issue for the wider community,
  was the growing rejection of the paternalism of the state and its
  professionals, and a need to redress the imbalance of power between
  the state and its agents and individuals and families engaged by the
  criminal justice system.*
- *Sixty years of paternalistic welfare legislation had little impact on
  levels of offending behaviour. Costly therapeutic programs that
  congregated young offenders, particularly in residential settings,
  emerged as part of the problem rather than part of the solution.*
- *Increasing numbers of young offenders were being sent to the adult
  court for sentence (over 2000 in 1988), an indication of the inability of
  the juvenile system to deal with them effectively.* (Consedine 1995,
  p.105)

Although this situation is similar to that in many countries, what has
subsequently occurred in Aotearoa/New Zealand has been profoundly unusual.
The new Labour Government of 1984 proposed legislation which met with
widespread criticism, especially from Maori and Pacific Island leadership.
When Labour was re-elected in 1987, a working party was formed that
consulted widely and particularly with Maori and Pacific Islander groups. The
result was the Children, Young Persons and Their Families Act of 1989.

Judge McElrea of the Auckland District Court describes the three
'distinctive - indeed revolutionary - elements of the Youth Court Model' that
have flowed from this legislation:

(i)   *The transfer of power from the State, principally the Courts' power,
       to the community.*
(ii)   *The Family Group Conference as a mechanism for producing a
       negotiated, community response.*
(iii) *The involvement of victims as key participants, making possible a
       healing process for both offender and victim.*
(McElrea 1995, p.2)

The following descriptions of the Family Group Conference process
have been informed by conversations with, and the writings of, Jim Consedine,
a prison chaplain since 1979 and co-ordinator of the National Movement for

Habilitation Centres and Restorative Justice.

Family group conferences

No longer are young offenders immediately arrested, charged and taken before the Children's or Young Offenders' Courts. In the vast majority of cases, after they have been apprehended by the police, they are returned to their families and, with considerable speed, a family group conference is arranged by the Youth Justice Co-ordinator of the area.

At the family group conference the young person who was apprehended committing an offence is invited, alongside his or her family and support people, to meet with the victim (or a representative nominated by the victim) and their support group. A facilitator, the police, and other professionals, are present - not to judge but to facilitate a process to assist the young person who committed the offence to recognise the damage done.

Generally the family of the young person who has been apprehended nominates the venue, which varies from family home, to church hall, to *marae*. There is no set formal procedure but often the co-ordinator, after introducing everyone, will read the police summary of facts. This can be challenged by the young person and may be amended on the spot. The young person suspected of the offence is then usually invited to respond. If they deny the allegations, the conference is adjourned to enable a Youth Court to be held. In the vast majority of cases they admit to the actions described and sometimes offer an explanation.

The victim is then invited to respond and the real impacts of the crime can be heard. If the victim has decided not to attend, their representative speaks on their behalf. The emotional consequences of robbery and other crimes often come as a complete shock to offenders. Within family group conferences, crimes are located back within relationships and people's lives. The process attempts to address emotional reactions to crime as opposed to simply proving guilt or innocence.

In a family group conference, unlike a courtroom, the offender must face the victim's family and speak of their remorse if they so choose. Another difference is that those who have experienced crime have a chance to speak in their own ways, to state the repercussions in a supportive context.

This process creates the possibilities for 'responsible reconciliation' and a reaching out across families and communities. Commonly the offender expresses remorse and gives some explanation for their actions. All those within the group conference contribute their ideas as to what would be an appropriate response.

The victim's views are obtained at that point. Usually they are interested in putting the wrong right, in reparation, in an apology, in having the young person come and work for them or a member of their family. Sometimes this conflicts with the police view (Consedine 1995, p.101).

The police give their opinions as to what would be appropriate, as do the co-ordinators. Then the young person who has committed the offence, and their family group, retire on their own. When they are ready they come back to announce what their proposal is in terms of a response to the situation. There are sometimes further negotiations if the police or the victim are not happy with the proposal, but usually there is agreement, and the chosen response becomes the offender's 'sentence' (Consedine 1995, p.102). Statistically the model has been extraordinarily successful:

Court appearances have plummeted. From a rate of something like 64 per 1000 young people appearing in court each year, it has dropped to 16. A third of young offenders used to appear in court. Now its only 10%, and the proportion who receive court orders has also decreased. (Consedine 1995, p.106)

Concerns

There are, however, some ongoing concerns. The role which professionals play in the conferences has been questioned: *In research covering the first three years of the process, in an average of 42 percent of cases the professionals did not leave the families alone to discuss a proposed penalty* (Consedine 1995, p.102). In the majority of cases, the background to the current offence is ignored (Consedine 1995, p.102). There are also concerns about the pressures that may be placed on young people to plead guilty, and about what can occur in these conferences if the young person is turned upon and retributive notions are applied. Some exponents of the system seem to have a faith in 'shaming' practices, but others have voiced concerns about them. Still others are concerned that the use of such models in cases of violent crimes may have adverse effects on the victims, and compromise their safety.

The power relations of families, communities and professionalism do not automatically vanish within alternative frameworks, and neither do cultural practices of retribution. However, many people believe that such an approach creates a context for the possibility of restoration and community building, which is very different from what is possible in conventional courtrooms. This is because power relations within the room are very different. There is a choice of whether or not to attend, loved ones are present providing support, and all those present at the conference have a right of veto which would take the case back into the formal system. As Jim Consedine describes:

> *People can be amazing when they are enmeshed in institutions that invite them to care about each other instead of hate each other ... The surprising thing is that victims, who so often call for more blood in traditional Western justice systems, in New Zealand frequently plead with the police to waive punishment and 'give the kid another chance'. Partly this happens because victims get an insight through the process of dialogue into the shocking life circumstances the young offender has had to confront.* (Consedine 1995, p.103)

Within such an alternative framework, those involved are invited into understanding and resolving conflicts and crime in the context of supportive relationships, and those who have experienced the crime play a central role in this.

Restorative justice

The Youth Court Model is part of a broader movement within Aotearoa/New Zealand, which is endeavouring to move away from 'retributive justice' and towards 'restorative justice': *Retributive justice always asks first, how do we punish the offender? Restorative justice asks, how do we restore the wellbeing of the victim, the community and the offender?* (Consedine 1995, back cover).

How can notions of 'restoration' be used without implying that 'normal' social circumstances are unquestionably harmonius and just, and should be restored? Is it possible to use such notions without ignoring structural injustices (Morris, R., in McElrea 1995, p.2)? Similarly, is it possible to effectively challenge the punitive notions of the criminal justice system without also including an analysis of class, race and gender oppression? And what exactly is meant by notions of 'wellbeing' or 'wellness'? I wonder how restorative ways of working can be generated in ways that empower communities, that involve grass-roots participation and decision-making. These questions refer, in many ways, to issues of accountability.

Questions of accountability

Those who are brought before family group conferences in Aotearoa/New Zealand and elsewhere are overwhelmingly young men from working-class communities, Indigenous communities, and communities of people of colour. It is hopeful and exciting that these young men will not be automatically confronted with the law courts, retribution, oppositional justice, and possible imprisonment. It is hopeful that processes will occur that have far greater hope of responsibility, both individual and collective, being built upon. It seems a positive step that family and community bonds are being strengthened in the process. And yet how will these processes be accountable to those communities most affected by their operation? And when these processes involve crimes of violence against women, how will they remain accountable to women within these communities? What will the role of professionals be?

A growing momentum to rebuild community

The Aotearoa/New Zealand Youth Court model is asking how processes of resolving conflict and crimes can be used to rebuild community relations in Western societies. As Judge Barry Stuart describes: *Resolving conflict is an essential building material of any relationship. Empowering communities to take responsibility for conflict within the community restores this essential building material of relationships within a community* (McElrea 1995, p.16).

Nils Christie speaks similarly: *Lawyers steal other people's conflicts: we need to give them back to the people directly concerned* (Swift 1996a, p.12).

In many other places there are similar developments taking place. Victim-offender mediation services, and other restorative justice initiatives, are taking hold in many different communities in North America, the UK, Australia, and continental Europe. Many of these programs share a determination to create community-building alternatives to prison (see Haley 1994, p.34).

Projects in which those who have experienced crime and offenders meet as an alternative to court (like the Aotearoa/New Zealand Youth Court Model) are now operating in many districts for both adults and young people

(Swift 1996b, p.29). Meetings between prisoners and victim advocacy groups are also increasing. In Vacaville, California, in 1988, male prisoners invited the Bay Area Women Against Rape (BAWAR) to speak to them and, after tentative beginnings, ongoing relationships were developed. Eight years on, the relationships continue with some prisoners volunteering to speak at schools and others serving as mediators in local victim/offender reconciliation projects (see Cvar 1996, p.54). There also seems to be the beginnings of a substantial shift in notions of crime prevention - away from a focus on protection and surveillance, and towards approaches based on rebuilding community relations (see van Gelder 1996, pp.16-22).

Reinventing the law

How these approaches may influence the law and legal systems is an interesting question. Within Aotearoa/New Zealand, the law itself has been written in the hope that its application will rebuild community links and relationships:

In the Children, Young Persons and their Families Act 1989 there is a clear statutory intention to attempt to strengthen families, church or school associations, sporting links and residential communities. (Judge M.L.A. Brown, in McElrea 1995, p.16)

Exploring the ways in which other forms of community building - support groups, consciousness raising and politicised community action groups - could be involved in these processes seems exciting. Perhaps our relationships to law will also be re-invented. Perhaps in the course of resolving crimes and conflicts within community relationships we will begin to live 'with the law' rather than under it. Perhaps the laws we choose to live by will be generated from and within relationships. Moana Jackson describes how this has always been the Maori way:

Law was not an isolated set of rules to be invoked only upon an infringement of accepted behavioural limits. Neither was it part of a distinct discipline to be 'learned' separately from the spiritual and religious beliefs of society. Instead it grew out of and was inextricably woven into the religious and hence everyday framework of Maori life. It reflected a special significance that was manifest in the spiritual ties of the people to their Gods, and the whakapapa *(genealogy) shared between individuals and the ancestors who bore them. The Maori lived not under the law but with it ... because individuals were inextricably linked by* whakapapa *to their* whanau *(extended family) and* iwi *(people), so were their actions the unavoidable responsibility of the wider group.* (paraphrased by Consedine 1995, p.92)

Note

1   *Marae* is the Maori term for community/spiritual meeting place.

19

Indigenous Australian justice

When we began, you'd never hear of an Aboriginal Death in Custody - now you do. It's in the papers and on the radio. But when was the last time you heard about a white death in custody? Nobody talks about that. Basically, as we keep saying to non-Aboriginal inmates in the jails, the Royal Commission recommendations will cover you as well as us. They can't have a two-tier system, they can't have a split system. And there definitely does need to be more work done on non-Aboriginal inmates. I, for the life of me, can't understand why there isn't an Asian body similar to ours, why there isn't a Muslim body similar to ours. For all I know, there bloody well may be, but they're certainly very, very low key.

Work needs to be done on all deaths in custody - ours are bad and so are non-Aboriginal deaths. I mean all deaths in jail are unnecessary. I don't doubt that non-Aboriginal people in jail receive similar treatment to what our people do. There's an argument about that, whether it's true or not, but I couldn't see the screws being nice to the non-Aboriginal inmates and only being crook against the Kooris. I'm sure they treat the Asians bad. I'm sure they treat the Muslims bad. All this sort of stuff. You'll never eliminate deaths in jail, you'll never eliminate violence, you'll never eliminate rape, but by Christ you can cut it down a hell of a lot. You can monitor it better and so decrease it. That's what our aim is. There's got to be concerted efforts by the non-Aboriginal groups to really put pressure on. (Ray Jackson, in conversation, 1996)

The above quotation comes from Ray Jackson, a member of the New South Wales Aboriginal Death in Custody Watch Committee. As he says, the fact that the issue of deaths in custody has been raised at all in this country, is due to the dedication and protest of Indigenous Australians. This is also true of most changes to prisons. Watch Committees now exist in every state:

> We see ourselves as an Aboriginal community group, working for and on the behalf of Aborigines in the custodial system, which covers of course the police, the prisons and the courts. But we also do a lot of what we call social justice work. We're on duty 24 hours a day, seven days a week. We get call-outs to police stations when they have juveniles there and they can't contact the parents for whatever reason. They can't interview them or do anything with them until an adult person is there, so they call us. We get called in by adults - cops ring up, so it's a growing amount of work. The more people learn of us, the heavier the work-load gets. (Ray Jackson, in conversation, 1996)

White Australian responses

The voices of Indigenous Australians offer a profound challenge to white Australia. They have been doing so for over two hundred years, as Kevin Gilbert describes:

> White society in this country hasn't changed all that much since the colonists first landed and began flogging the convicts. Remember your history books when an incident like that occurred and the Aboriginals who came up recoiled in horror, screaming frantically and throwing sticks at the soldiers and the flogger? Remember do you? It hasn't changed all that much. And no, you haven't grown in stature to match this country yet. You are still the alien, the outsider and only when you embrace the whole of this country, every sacred living thing upon it and in it and around it, will you grow and survive, because only those who love the land and love justice will ultimately hold the land. (Gilbert 1977)

What is it within white culture that restrains us from taking action on issues of prisons and punishment? What is it that prevents us in our own lives from being outraged about deaths in custody? And what will it take for us in our own lives and as a culture to slowly rebuild community links and relationships in ways that address crimes and conflict?

In July 1996, sitting around a table at Looma, a small Indigenous Australian community south-west of Derby in north-west Australia, the conversation turned to deaths in custody. After talking at some length about the attempts of Indigenous Australians to bring about change in this area, and sharing information about the latest developments regarding the implementation of the findings of the Royal Commission into Aboriginal Deaths in Custody, one member of the community turned to us with a question: 'What does the white community do when a young white person dies in custody?' It was asked with genuine curiosity and with the hope of learning something from our attempts to bring about justice and prevent the deaths of young white Australians in prisons.

When we tried to answer that the white community pays little attention to white deaths in custody, that they occur with little or no public protest, and that there is not a sense of outrage within our communities, a look of complete puzzlement came over his face. He was simply bewildered over how a people could not care for their young men and women to such an extent that they could die within institutions of degradation and no-one would make a noise, no-one would care. For the rest of the meeting he remained disbelieving - how could it be?

Community alternatives to the Police

Within many Indigenous communities further developments are occurring in establishing alternatives to the police, and instituting culturally appropriate responses to crimes. Earlier chapters described the role of the police in the colonisation and ongoing persecution of Indigenous Australians. In response to this situation, in many cities, including Broome, Derby and Alice Springs, Indigenous Australians have established their own 'night patrols'. These patrols act as the first point of call for disturbances within their communities and seek to reduce the role of the police. They are often co-ordinated by local land councils and are generally run by Indigenous Australian men and women who have experienced the mainstream criminal 'justice' system and wish to provide an alternative.

This task is far from easy or uncomplicated, especially when one considers the history within this country of white Australians setting Indigenous Australians against each other - a history that includes recruiting Indigenous

Australians to police and track down other Indigenous Australians.

Two of the key questions that many of the night patrols are exploring are: how much to involve mainstream services and institutions, such as hospitals or the police force; and how to create alternative institutions which are grassroots organisations that are accountable to their communities and run in culturally appropriate ways. Within Derby, at present, the night patrol involves the police and the lock-up in situations of physical disturbances, because to return a person to their home in a violent and/or drunken state may only be moving the problem around rather than in any way addressing it. The longer term hope is to have an Indigenous Australian shelter established so that the police need not be involved in matters to do with the Indigenous Australian communities. To even be thinking of such a possibility represents just how far night patrols have come.

The Indigenous Australian example of communities responding to and dealing with their own seems again to offer an invitation to white Australians: An invitation to find other ways of resolving crime and conflict within our communities rather than leaving it to anonymous outsiders: An invitation to create alternative responses to the dominant traditions of policing which have been so influenced by notions of masculinity, punishment, and military-style structures. Such invitations have already begun to be taken up by police in some contexts. If we were to take them up all over this country, what would it mean for white, middle-class Australians like myself? If we were ever the victims of crime, would we seek out these alternative paths, rather than relying on conventional notions of punishment and retribution? And what might these alternative paths look like? Indigenous Australian communities again provide some examples.

Cultural and community rebuilding

Wallace Rockhole is a small Indigenous Australian community south-west of Alice Springs. It is now a place of Indigenous Australian pride and culture, and each year thousands of people from around the world visit to walk upon its land and hear its stories. What is perhaps most remarkable is that its resurgence was built largely upon responses to issues of crime and alcoholism. Young men who were in trouble with the law were brought to Wallace Rockhole when all that existed there was an out-station. They began to reconnect with their culture and learn the ways of the land. Once there, often they did not want to leave, and slowly the community was reborn. Wallace

Rockhole stands as testimony to what can be achieved when community-building and reconnection to culture replaces individualistic and punitive approaches to crime.

Ray Jackson, of the Sydney Aboriginal Deaths in Custody Watch Committee, points to a similar development occurring within New South Wales:

Our people have to get in touch with their own culture, their own ways of living as we see it should be. Funnily enough, Corrective Services have come up with the same things and they are now looking to purchase stations (up to $300,000), initially in western New South Wales, which they will then offer to the local Aboriginal community to operate and manage for them. What they are seeking is a place that can hold about twenty to thirty inmates, a working station run by Kooris for Koori offenders. They'll only take people from out of that far-western area so, instead of going to Broken Hill jail, twenty people can go out to this working station. They've got to be people with less than twelve months to go, which basically means they are low security, and of course kids.

It's good, great, to help them get in touch with their lands, 'cause out there it's their country. And we support that 100%, and in fact we say that's number one. Now where's the rest? Because there's other Koori-owned stations and they could be used for identical purposes. In fact I know that locals tried for years to get Juvenile Justice to send kids there instead of down to Sydney. Let them stay up there on their own country, where their parents can come in and visit them. They've got all that family support, it's a working station on their land, and they can get in touch with their culture, their elders. It's starting to change. (in conversation, 1996)

20

Towards alternative responses
to men's violence

The approaches outlined in the previous chapters are community responses to crime that are, in their very process, community-building. In such approaches, there are several issues which are seen as being more important than the final sentence or penalty. These are the processes of identifying conflicts between people as community, rather than individual, issues, and using community focused strategies to address them. In doing this, it is of prime concern that the safety of those involved is ensured, and that further harm is prevented. Rather than conforming to uniform penalties as a response, creative solutions are sought in individual situations. The responses seek not to replicate domination, and the processes occur within, and are run by, the community most affected by the events they are dealing with, and those who experience crime play an important role.

When discussing these approaches, and ways of learning from them, there are often questions asked in relation to issues of men's violence: How could these processes ensure the safety of the survivors of men's violence? How could they remain accountable to women in the communities where the violence had taken place? How could the voices of survivors be honoured within these processes?

Rosemary Couch[1] is the co-ordinator of Circle Justice at Whitehorse in the Yukon, Northern Canada. In the following interview she discusses the ways in which these issues are being addressed in Circle Justice settings in the

Yukon. The following piece is an edited version of an interview which took place in Whitehorse in April 1996:

It is in relation to issues of domestic violence and our victim services that we clash the most with sections of the community here in Whitehorse, because it's a different thinking, it's a different mentality. The community really believe that a lot of people become victims of past cycles, because of past learned behaviours, because of things they've become used to. The formal system will say, 'Well, you're re-victimising them'. That's the criticism we get. We try to be really aware of the whole process. We have a whole focus on getting people that are victimised into a survivor type of role rather than remaining in a victim perspective, because they just may end up continuing that cycle. Even if we deal with one man, say in a physical abuse situation, they'll end up with another one, or they'll go back to him. So that's something that the community really recognises, and yet the formal justice system says we're wrong, that model doesn't work, you don't do that, it's wrong, wrong, wrong! So we end up with a lot of conflict there.

The way the process is working now is that, as soon as the offender comes into a program and/or a victim requests that an offender be sentenced in the program process, then what will happen is that the victim co-ordinator is responsible for ensuring that the victim's needs and concerns are addressed throughout the whole process. The victim co-ordinator is from the community, she's very grassroots, somebody who everybody can trust and relate to. From the time the offender comes in she'll begin to ensure that he is considering the victims, asking: 'How do you think the victim feels about this?' and so on. She'll make contact with the victim and talk to the victim and invite the victim in for lay counselling, to talk to somebody for support. If the person doesn't want to have any involvement in circle sentencing then she'll do an impact statement.

There are a number of things that happen. There's no set right way that can help the victim. Often we have victims come to circle and that's very powerful, a powerful process for an offender to hear the harm that they have created in that person's life, for the family to recognise what their son or daughter has done to another family. It's just amazing the dynamics that happen when they are there. When they are not there, you still get the victim issues and concerns in the circle.

We have a women's support group and a men's support group, and both victims and offenders are encouraged, if they are comfortable, to attend that group. They meet on different nights once a week. If anything, it's as much an opportunity for a victim to become engaged as it is for the offender to become re-engaged in the community. So we see a lot of women all of a sudden participating in women's camps and getting re-connected with the community, whereas before they have been really isolated.

In relation to the perpetrators, it is a person-by-person approach, and I don't think that these processes are panaceas. I've got to be honest: for a long period of time, one of our criteria was that we didn't accept sexual offenders. And there was a number of reasons for that. We needed to ensure that we were dealing with this in the right way, that we had the appropriate resources to deal with it, that the community was ready to move on it, that the training was there, and the strength was there to carry it out.

We are doing our first sexual-abuse-related case right now, and it's going to be sentenced in May, and the community has just come unglued. We had been warned about this by people in other projects going on in Canada. They said: 'Well, are you ready to take on your first sexual-related case? Be prepared for the community to go'. And that's been happening. This case is the first case that I've had to be responsible for walking through the process, and I've felt extremely comfortable in doing this, because all we're doing is improving dramatically what the formal justice system is trying to do.

This person that we are working with now has got about 15 people involved in his life. His support group is very big. The community is completely aware. There is just a number of very good checks and balances in place, and this person is extremely motivated. He's very honest, he's very open about the fact that he knows what's going on in his head, he knows that he can be dangerous. I think we have to get over that in a lot of ways. We don't just automatically assume that all people or situations are suitable for these processes. We just know that the current process needs to improve, because these people are still coming back into our communities and they are often in re-offending cycles again. What we are trying to do is improve what's happening dramatically and get the community taking ownership.

The whole community knows who he is now. You know, they watch him, they see what he is doing. According to our traditional ways, you wear a feather in your hat until you've made your wrong-doing right.

That's pretty well the summary: 'You've done wrong. It doesn't mean you're a bad person, but you have to make it right.' So probably in a year from now when he's gone through this process and he's addressed his issues, he'll be demonstrating his own stuff to the community.

I think what's important is that this is not a procedural aspect we're going through. It's very, very human right from the beginning. And through it, people's true colours come out and that's the beauty of it. You can walk in to a lawyer who you don't know and you can portray anything you want, but when your aunts, sisters, brothers, cousins, family, relatives, boss and everybody else is sitting there, your true colours come through. They know when you're not ready, when you are actually a threat to the community. They know it. I think that's the only hope, that the person is then accountable to the community, and the community is giving them a chance. Most people need to be connected to the community. The need to have a purpose in the community, the need to belong is very strong, so when the community gives them a chance, most people will take it.

I've been through a family violence situation myself, and there's a lot of women who sit in the circle when we have a family violence case come through, and what will happen is complete consensus will take place. So many women have experienced this, and the circle is an opportunity to share it with the community. It's an opportunity to address it as a community issue and not as an individual hide-it-in-the-closet issue. Women are saying the same thing: they want their power back, they want the abuse to stop, they want healthy relationships. Now how do they get to that when they are so used to other ways, and how do you get a man to change behaviours that may be so ingrained? We don't know. The cases we've done have been really good, we've had extreme success with them, we haven't had a re-offence in a family violence situation, but that's maybe six cases, so we haven't had enough experience with it.

So we debate, we struggle with these questions, but again all we can do is try to have enough people involved in the process when we are working through those issues. As our foundation, we know we aren't going to leave them worse off than they already were, we know we can't do worse than what the formal system has done to our people. It's a process of trusting the community.

Talking about ways beyond

The devastating effects of men's violence make it very difficult to consider it an area in which to explore alternative approaches. This is especially so when, with male violence already trivialised in the culture, the alternatives to incarceration that are often proposed overwhelmingly deny the seriousness of men's violence, the need for a strong and committed community response, and the need for responsibility to be taken and safety assured. The most common forms of alternatives exist within the framework of the current legal system and often tap into understandings of men's violence that have the effect of excusing this behaviour, denying its effects, and/or silencing the links to issues of masculinity, gender and power. Often the alternatives proposed are those of therapy, and many feminists have asked serious questions about both the accountability of these processes and the politics of individualising this abuse and obscuring what is a community issue.

On the other hand, perhaps the more serious the offence, the more an alternative, community-building and restorative approach is required. It may also be true that, at times of profound grief, outrage and anger, perhaps the least healing response is that which is offered by the police, courts and prison - confrontation and retribution.

These issues raise many questions: What sort of immediate community responses would offer greater protection for those at risk of men's violence? What responses would encourage men to take responsibility for their actions, rather than a legal process that encourages denial, defensiveness and opposition? For those men from whom women and children need protection, what sort of processes (institutions?) that don't replicate domination could be created? And how could addressing such questions be linked to the process of rebuilding communities within this culture?

Turning to the big picture too quickly seems a recipe for either despair or reverting to dominating and degrading ·practices. Addressing issues of domestic violence and sexual violence is the biggest challenge for alternative frameworks, just as it is within the mainstream system.

Any efforts to deal with men's violence will ripple into issues of prison, and as we try to find ways to talk about prisons and their effects on individuals, communities and our culture, every conversation will invite us to consider new community responses to men's violence.

As the WOWSafe women stated in earlier chapters, the police, courts and prisons have generally been unsuccessful in responding to men's violence. They also point to the ways in which it has been women who have reached out to one another, reduced the isolation of violent situations, turned up on the doorsteps of men who are violent, and involved local neighbourhoods in responding. Within the alternative ways in which women have historically resisted men's violence, and supported one another, there may be the foundations for change.

Putting the dilemmas, outrage, hopes and sorrow out into the world, on paper and in conversations, is a good place to start. Sharing our experiences in this way may help break down the isolation so often felt by people struggling with these issues, and provide a context in which new partnerships may be created. Such new partnerships could then, perhaps, enable us to step out into the unknown.

Note

1. Rosemary Couch is the co-ordinator of Circle Justice sentencing in Whitehorse, in the Yukon in Northern Canada, and can be contacted c/- the Community Social Justice Program, Kwanlin Oun First Nation, PO Box 1217, Whitehorse YT, Canada, YCA 5AS.

End note

At first glance, the current culture of imprisonment appears to be growing stronger. Increasing numbers of men and women are being locked away, for longer and longer sentences, and in newer and larger prisons. And yet, as described in this book, there are rich alternative traditions upon which to build, both here in this country and elsewhere.

My mind flashes to songs deep within prison walls, to the daily acts of resistance, to those who care, to those who dare to speak, to those who survive another day marked off on a calendar. In concert with these people are Indigenous Australians, vocal in their resistance to deaths in custody and imprisonment as a tool of colonisation. From here to the circles of the Yukon, to *marae* justice, to the creation of new courtrooms and new ways of working, there are powerful foundations on which to build. The communities most affected by imprisonment seem to be lighting new ways forward, creating the possibility of weeding out notions of punishment from our beings, from our institutions of degradation, and from our cities.

This country was invaded to become a prison, not only for the Indigenous Peoples, but also for the poor of Britain. Now, over two hundred years after this country was invaded to become a prison, cracks are beginning to appear in the culture of imprisonment, cracks caused by generations of protest.

This book is part of a broader project to break the cultural silences that surround prisons and imprisonment. As I look back over these pages, I have the sense of a gathering together of dreams. The sorrow and outrage about prisons that have at times eaten away at my spirit are now somehow balanced by the belief that we will find ways beyond incarceration.

Over the past months, I have begun to get in contact with my own history of protest against prison, my own sense of uncomfortableness and contradictions. Through finding ways and places in which to share these stories, and in listening to the struggles and experiences of others, I am sensing a movement, one that is founded on the world re-imagined. Possibilities are being created and, all the while, the words of Antonia Machado act as a gentle reminder: *Traveller, there is no road; one makes the road by walking* (Swift 1996b, p.30).

About the contributors

Rosemary Couch is the co-ordinator of Circle Justice sentencing in Whitehorse, in the Yukon, Northern Canada. She can be contacted c/- Community Social Justice Program, Kwanlin Oun First Nation, PO Box 1217, Whitehorse YT, YCA 5AS, Canada.

David Denborough was employed to work within the New South Wales prison system from 1993 to 1996, firstly as a welfare worker, and then as a part-time teacher of social welfare and 'life skills'. Over the same period, with Sydney Men Against Sexual Assault, he worked in schools with young men on issues of masculinity and violence. David has recently moved back to the home of his childhood, Canberra, ACT, Australia, where he hopes to continue working in schools, writing, playing music, and taking long walks in the mountains.

Clint Deveaux has been a municipal court judge in Atlanta, Georgia, since 1981, and is nationally known throughout North America as an advocate of accountability based alternatives to incarceration. Clint can be contacted at the Atlanta Municipal Court, 170 Garnett Street SW, Atlanta Georgia 30303-3612, USA, telephone: (404) 8658104.

Suzanne Elliott, a community activist, has been working actively for social change in Adelaide, South Australia, since 1983, with a particular focus on women's politics; supporting Aboriginal self-determination struggles; anti-racism work; and supporting other liberation struggles. Suzanne was a member of the organising collective of the Adelaide-based group of women who organised 'Women and Political Action Forums', in 1988, which was a city-wide women's action group. Suzanne can be contacted c/- The Aboriginal and Multicultural Women's Project, 85 Hookings Terrace, Woodville Gardens SA 5012, Australia.

Eddie Ellis is a former member of the Black Panther party, and a survivor of the Attica insurrection. After serving 23 years in prison, he is now developing a prisoner education, research and advocacy organisation called the Community Justice Centre in the village of Harlem, New York. Eddie, and others involved in the Non-Traditional Approach to Criminal and Social Justice, can be contacted c/- Community Justice Center, 1825 Park Avenue, Room 604, New York NY 10035, USA, telephone (212) 427 4545.

Harold Gatensky lives outside of Carcross in the Yukon, Northern Canada. He has been involved in circle justice initiatives within his community and within prisons for many years. He can be contacted c/- Rosemary Couch (as above).

Sharon Gollan has worked in various organisations to assist Indigenous Australians in their struggle for social justice. She is a strong activist in the fight against all forms of racism which many of her people are confronted with daily in their lives, and is currently facilitating 'challenging racism' workshops for various organisations in South Australia, and also in other Australian states. Sharon can be contacted c/- Dulwich Centre, Hutt St PO Box 7192, Adelaide SA 5000, Australia.

Blanche Hampton, a prison activist and author, lives in Sydney, Australia. Her publications include *Prisons and Women,* and *No Escape: Prisons, therapy and politics* (see References).

Ray Jackson is the current Management Committee Co-ordinator of the Aboriginal Deaths in Custody Watch Committee Inc. The Watch Committee is an organisation formed in Sydney during June 1987 to protest the large number of deaths of Indigenous Australians in custody. Ray can be contacted c/- PO Box 65, Broadway NSW 2007, Australia.

Sheridan Linnell has worked for many years as a therapist and consultant with women and children who have experienced men's violence. She is the co-author, with Dorothy Cora, of *Discoveries: A group resource guide for women who have been sexually abused in childhood* (see References). Sheridan can be contacted c/- PO Box 42, Lawson NSW 2783, Australia.

Mishka Lysack, in addition to being a therapist in the Young Offender Unit at the Ottowa-Carleton Detention Center, has a practice of doing and teaching therapy in Ottowa, Canada. His ideas do not necessarily represent those of the Ministry of Solicitor-General and Correctional Services of Ontario, Canada. Mishka can be contacted c/- Young Offender Unit, 2244 Innes Road, Gloucester, Ont., K1B 4C4, Canada.

Trevor Pugh worked for seven years for the South Australian Correctional Services, and now wants to stop the cycle by helping young offenders stay out of the prison system. Trevor can be contacted c/- PO Box 1454, Murray Bridge SA 5253, Australia.

Gaye Stockell & Marilyn O'Neill are committed to participating in 'enabling' conversations with people who find themselves in 'disabling' contexts. They have recently set up a narrative centre and offer therapy consultations, worker co-visioning, and narrative workshops. Marilyn and Gaye can be contacted c/- the Collaborative Consultation Centre, 32A Ridge St, North Sydney NSW 2060, Australia.

Pia van de Zandt has been working as a Research/Policy Officer at the Department for Women in Sydney, Australia, on issues of law and violence, for over two years. After being interviewed for this book she decided that she had lost all her cred and was verging on being sucked into the big bad bureaucracy forever. So she began to plan her escape. Pia has managed to con her mate into going away with her to Holland where she will work for a couple of years in one of the biggest bureaucracies of all the world.

Women and Political Action Forums (see Suzanne Elliott this section).

WOWSafe (Women of the West for Safe Families) is a group of women who have survived spouse abuse, who have formed themselves into an action group at The Parks Community Health Service, Angle Park SA 5010, Australia. Their Sister System helps other women and children in crisis. They lobby parliament, government departments, and other agencies, to promote legislation and practices aimed at increasing safety for women and children, and also speak to community and professional groups to raise awareness in the community about family violence.

References

Aboriginal Health Council of South Australia, 1995:
'Reclaiming Our Stories, Reclaiming Our Lives.' *Dulwich Centre Newsletter*, No.1.

Abu-Jamal, M. 1995:
Live From Death Row. New York: Addison-Wesley.

Acoli, 1995:
'A Brief History of the New Afrikan Prison Struggle.' *NOBO Journal Of African American Dialogue*, 2(1):1-2, special issue: 'Black Prison Movements USA'. New Jersey: Africa World Press.

Anderson, T. 1992:
Take Two: The Criminal Justice System Revisited. Sydney: Bantam.

Aronoff, B.R. 1991:
Dead Man Walking: A Matter of Time. Red Bluff, CA: Eagle Publishing.

Atkinson, L. 1995:
'Boot Camps and Justice: A contradiction in terms?' *Trends and Issues in Crime and Criminal Justice*, No.46. Canberra: Australian Institute of Criminology.

Baker, J. 1993:
'Aboriginal Health Issues Within the Disease System.' *Social Alternatives*, 12(1):41-44.

Bennett, L. 1995:
'Our Home, Our Land.' Compact disc, *Our Home, Our Land: Something to sing about*. Alice Springs, Northern Territory, Australia: CAAMA Music.

Billy, Fred & Eddie, 1994:
'Black in a White Man's World.' *XY: Men, Sex, Politics*, 4(3):14-15.

Christie, N. 1993:
Crime Control as Industry. London: Routledge.

Churchill, W. 1992:
'The Third World at Home: Political prisons and prisoners in the United States.' In Churchill, W. & Vander Wall, J.J. (eds), *Cages of Steel: The Politics of Imprisonment in the United States*. Washington DC: Maisonneuve Press.

Churchill, W. & Vander Wall, J.J. (eds) 1992:
Cages of Steel: The Politics of Imprisonment in the United States. Washington DC: Maisonneuve Press.

Consedine, J. 1995:
  Restorative Justice: Healing the Effects of Crime. Christchurch, NZ: Ploughshares Publications.
Cvar, J. 1996:
  'Transformation: Victim Offender Reconciliation.' *In Context*, No.38, p.54.
Dann, C. 1991:
  'In Love With The Land.' In King, M. (ed), *Pakeha: The Quest for Identity in New Zealand.* Auckland, NZ: Penguin.
Davidson, H.S. (ed) 1995:
  Schooling in a Total Institution: Critical Perspectives on Prison Education. London: Bergin & Garvey.
Denborough, D. 1995:
  'Step by Step: Developing respectful and effective ways of working with young men to reduce violence.' *Dulwich Centre Newsletter*, Nos.2&3.
Donaldson, S. 1994:
  'Hooking Up: Protective pairing for punks.' Handout from *Stop Prisoner Rape*, PO Box 2713 Manhattanville Sta, New York NY 10027-8817, USA.
Donaldson, S. 1995:
  'Rape of Incarcerated Americans: A preliminary statistical look.' Handout from *Stop Prisoner Rape*, PO Box 2713 Manhattanville Sta, New York NY 10027-8817, USA.
Egan, T. 1994:
  'Thinking in Australian.' In Graham, D. (ed), *Being Whitefella.* South Fremantle, Western Australia: Fremantle Arts Centre Press.
Elijah, J.S. 1995:
  'Conditions of Confinement - Cruel and Unusual Punishment for Black Political Prisoners.' *The NOBO Journal of African American Dialogue*, 2(1):137-148, special issue: 'Black Prison Movements USA'. New Jersey: Africa World Press.
Elliot, 1994:
  'Whenever I Tell You the Language We Use is a Class Issue, You Nod Your Head in Agreement - and Then You Open Your Mouth.' In Penelope, J. (ed.), *Out of the Class Closet: Lesbians Speak.* Freedom, CA: The Crossing Press.
Ellis, E. 1995:
  'Non-Traditional Approach to Criminal and Social Justice.' *The NOBO Journal of African American Dialogue*, 2(1):92-105, special issue: 'Black Prison Movements USA'. New Jersey: Africa World Press.
Epston, D. & White, M. 1990:
  'Consulting Your Consultants: The documentation of alternative knowledges.' In Epston, D. & White, M., *Experience, Contradiction, Narrative & Imagination.* Adelaide, South Australia: Dulwich Centre Publications.
Faith, K. 1993:
  Unruly Women: The Politics of Confinement and Resistance. Vancouver: Press Gang Publishers.
Foucault, M. 1977:
  Discipline and Punish: The Birth of the Prison. London: Penguin.
Gilbert, K. 1977:
  Living Black. Ringwood, Victoria: Allen Lane, Penguin Press.

Graham, D. (ed) 1994:
  Being Whitefella. South Fremantle, Western Australia: Fremantle Arts Centre Press.
Greven, P. 1992:
  Spare the Child.: The Religious Roots of Punishment and the Psychological Impact of Physical Abuse. New York: Vintage Books.
Grieves, L. 1996:
  'Reflections.' *Revive*, 2(1):12-13.
Haley, J. 1994:
  'Victim-Offender Mediation: International success.' *In Context*, No.38, p.34.
Hampton, B. 1993:
  Prisons and Women. Sydney: University of New South Wales Press.
Hampton, B. 1994:
  No Escape: Prisons, Therapy and Politics. Sydney: University of New South Wales Press.
Heilpern , D. 1994:
  'Sexual Assault of New South Wales Prisoners.' Paper delivered at *10th Annual Conference of the Australian and New Zealand Society of Criminology*, 28th September, University of New South Wales.
hooks, bell, 1994:
  Outlaw Culture. New York: Routledge.
Horii, G.K. 1994:
  'The Art in/of Survival.' *Journal of Prisoners on Prison*, 5(2):6-8.
Howe, A. 1994:
  Punish and Critique: Towards a Feminist Analysis of Penality. London: Routledge.
Hughes, R. 1988:
  The Fatal Shore. London: Pan Books.
Jackson, M. 1990:
  'Criminality and the Exclusion of Maori.' In Cameron, N. & France, S. (eds), *Essays on Criminal Law in New Zealand - Towards Reform*. Wellington, NZ: Victoria University Press.
Jenkins, A. 1990:
  Invitations to Responsibility: The Therapeutic Engagement of Men who are Violent and Abusive. Adelaide, South Australia: Dulwich Centre Publications
King, M. (ed) 1991:
  Pakeha: The Quest for Identity in New Zealand. Auckland, NZ: Penguin.
Kurshan, N. 1995:
  'Women and Imprisonment in the US: History and Current Reality.' In Rosenblatt, E. (ed), *With the Power of Justice in Our Eyes: A Handbook for Educators and Activists on the Crisis in Prisons*. Berkeley, CA: Prison Activist Resource Center.
Lewis, C.S. 1961:
  The Screwtape Letters and Screwtape Purposes. New York: MacMillan.
Lichtenstein, A.C. & Kroll, M.A. 1995:
  'The Fortress Economy: The economic role of the US prison system.' In Rosenblatt, E. (ed), *With the Power of Justice in Our Eyes: A Handbook for Educators and Activists on the Crisis in Prisons*. Berkeley, CA: Prison Activist Resource Center.

Linnell, S. & Cora, D. 1993:
   Discoveries: A Group Resource Guide for Women Who Have Been Sexually Abused in Childhood. Sydney, Australia: Dympna House Publications.
Lysack, M. 1996:
   'Inside the Panoptican: Doing therapy within a prison.' Unpublished paper. Ottowa, Canada.
Mauer, M. 1995:
   'Americans Behind Bars: One year later.' In Rosenblatt, E. (ed), *With the Power of Justice in Our Eyes: A Handbook for Educators and Activists on the Crisis in Prisons.* Berkeley, CA: Prison Activist Resource Center.
McCulloch, J. 1995:
   'Women, Prison, Law and Order.' *Women and Imprisonment.* Melbourne, Australia: Fitzroy Legal Service.
McElrea, F.W.M. 1995:
   'Accountability in the Community: Taking responsibility for offending.' Paper at *Legal Research Foundation Conference: Re-thinking Criminal Justice: A Conference on New Initiatives in Criminal Justice.* Auckland, New Zealand.
McEwen, C. 1994:
   'Growing Up Upper Class.' In Penelope, J. (ed), *Out of the Class Closet: Lesbians speak.* Freedom, CA: The Crossing Press.
McLean, C. 1995:
   'Speaking Out from the Dominant Position.' *Comment,* No.2.
Messerschmidt, J.W. 1993:
   Masculinities and Crime: Critique and Reconceptualization of Theory. Maryland, USA: Rowman & Littlefield Publishers.
Mukherjee, S. & Dagger, D. 1993:
   Australian Prisoners 1993: Results of National Prison Census. Canberra: Australian Institute of Criminology.
Outlook, P. 1994:
   'Gay Behind Bars.' X*Y: Men, Sex, Politics*, 4(3).
Penelope, J. 1994:
   'Class and Consciousness.' In Penelope, J. (ed.), *Out of the Class Closet: Lesbians Speak.* Freedom, CA: The Crossing Press.
Pike, D. 1994:
   'Freedom Lost.' *XY: Men, Sex, Politics,* 4(3):17.
Pilger, J. 1992:
   'The White Man's Tune.' In Pilger, J., *Distant Voices.* London: Vintage.
Prejean, H. 1993:
   Dead Man Walking. New York: Vintage Books.
Prison Activist Resource Center & California Coalition for Battered Women in Prison, 1995:
   'Self Defense is Not a Crime: Some facts on domestic violence.' In Rosenblatt, E. (ed), *With the Power of Justice in Our Eyes: A Handbook for Educators and Activists on the Crisis in Prisons.* Berkeley, CA: Prison Activist Resource Center.
Prison Research Education Action Project, 1976:
   Instead of Prisons: Handbook for Abolitionists. Syracuse, New York.

Rosenblatt, E. (ed) 1995:
With the Power of Justice in Our Eyes: A Handbook for Educators and Activists on the Crisis in Prisons. Berkeley, CA: Prison Activist Resource Center.
Royal Commission into Aboriginal Deaths in Custody [1987-1990] 1991:
'National Report' by Commissioner Elliott Johnston (5 volumes). Canberra, ACT: Australian Government Printer. (Parliamentary Papers Nos.126-130 of 1991.)
Royal Commission into New South Wales Prisons [1976-1978] 1978:
'Report of the Royal Commission into New South Wales Prisons' (3 volumes). Sydney, Australia: Government Printer. (Parliamentary Paper No.322 of 1976-77-78.)
Ryan, M. 1995:
'Solitude as Counterinsurgency - The US Isolation Model of Political Incarceration.' In Churchill, W. & Vander Wall, J.J. (eds), *Cages of Steel: The Politics of Imprisonment in the United States.* Washington DC: Maisonneuve Press.
Scott, R. 1991:
'The Trick of Standing Upright.' In King, M. (ed), *Pakeha: The Quest for Identity in New Zealand.* Auckland, NZ: Penguin.
Shakur, M., Bradshaw, A., Dinguswa, M., Long, T., Cook, M., Matos, A. & Haskins, J. 1995:
'Primer to Counterinsurgency and Low Intensity Warfare: Genocide through behaviour modification in the US penal system.' *The NOBO Journal of African American Dialogue,* 2(1):92-105, special issue: 'Black Prison Movements USA. New Jersey: Africa World Press.
Somebody's Daughter Theatre Company, 1994:
Call My Name. Melbourne, Australia: Somebody's Daughter Theatre Inc.
Stir-Fry Productions, 1991:
The Color of Fear. 90min film/video. California.
Summers, A. 1994:
Damned Whores and God's Police, 2nd edn. Victoria, Australia: Penguin.
Swift, R. 1996a:
'Crime and Civilisation.' *New Internationalist,* No.282.
Swift, R. 1996b:
'A Way Out.' *New Internationalist,* No.282.
Vander Wall, J.J. 1992:
'The Death Penalty and the Supreme Court: A case-study in American democracy.' In Churchill, W. & Vander Wall, J.J. (eds), *Cages of Steel: The Politics of Imprisonment in the United States.* Washington DC: Maisonneuve Press.
van Gelder, S. 1995:
'The Ecology of Justice: Making connections to stop crime.' *In Context,* No.38.
van Gelder (ed) 1996:
'Roots in Community.' *In Context,* No.38, pp.16-22.
van Ness, D.W., Carlson, D.R., Crawford, T. & Strong, K. 1994:
'A Short History of Justice.' *In Context,* No.38, p.13.
Wayne & Cheryl, 1996:
'Wayne and Cheryl.' *Polare,* No.12, pp.12-13.

White, M. & Epston, D. 1990:
  Narrative Means to Therapautic Ends. New York: WWNorton.
White, M. 1991:
  'Deconstruction and Therapy.' *Dulwich Centre Newsletter,* No.3, pp.21-40.
Women and Imprisonment Group, 1995:
  Women and Imprisonment. Melbourne, Australia: Fitzroy Legal Service.